ƒP

Other Works
by David Mamet

Some Freaks

Writing in Restaurants

The Village

On Directing Film

The Cabin

Make-Believe Town

Three Uses of the Knife

Passover

True and False

The Old Religion

Other Works
by David Mamet

Some Freaks

Writing in Restaurants

The Village

On Directing Film

The Cabin

Make-Believe Town

Three Uses of the Knife

Passover

True and False

The Old Religion

Jafsie and John Henry

Essays | David Mamet

The Free Press

fP

THE FREE PRESS
A Division of Simon & Schuster Inc.
1230 Avenue of the Americas
New York, NY 10020

THE FREE PRESS and colophon are trademarks
of Simon & Schuster Inc.

Designed by Carla Bolte

Manufactured in the United States of America

10 9 8 7 6 5 4 3 2 1

Library of Congress Cataloging-in-Publication Data

Mamet, David.
    Jafsie and John Henry : essays / David Mamet
      p. cm.
    ISBN 0-684-84120-7
    I. Title.
    PS3563.A4345J34   1999
    814'.54—dc21   98-49040
                                     CIP

The following essays have been published previously (in slightly different forms):
"Salad Days" (*Grand Street*, 1998); "Black Cashmere Sweater" ("Diary of a Sweater,"
Esquire, 1996); "Six Hours of Perfect Poker" ("The Last Hand," *Men's Journal*, 1995);
"Scotch Malt Whisky Society" ("Scotch," *Playboy*, 1996); "Knives" (*Men's Journal*,
1998-99); "Caps" ("Mad Hatters," *Esquire*, 1996); "Producers" (*Black Book*, 1998); "L.A.
Homes" (*Los Angeles Times*, 1996); "Karmann Ghia" (*Black Book*, 1997); "Smash Cut"
(*Scenario*, 1995); "The Screenplay and the State Fair," (*Zoetrope*, 1998); "Bad Boys"
(*Black Book*, 1998); "Resorts" (*Esquire*, 1996); "Noach" (*Genesis As It Is Written*, Harper-
Collins, 1996); "Race Driving School" (*Travel and Leisure*, 1998); "Domicile" (*Architec-
tural Digest*, 1996); "Late Season Hunt" (*Sports Afield*, 1998).

To Shel

Contents

Jafsie and John Henry

Introduction

I do not know how I escaped becoming a criminal.

All my life, as long as I can remember, I've had a recur-
ring dream. In the dream I have killed someone. I tell myself, in the dream, that I have had this dream before, that
the murder is not real, that it is, again, just a dream. Then
a sense of reality overcomes me, and I know past cer-
tainty that this time the dream is real, that I have killed,
and all the world is against me.

Police in airports, customs officials, border guards seem
to find me interesting. I feel or see their double take or
turn, and I sigh remarking it—which, I am sure, further
confirms their instincts or suspicions. The sigh is seen as
an admission of guilty knowledge, but the truth is more
benign. They are simply looking at someone who knows
he does not belong.

This is a perhaps overly nice rendition of the situation
of the writer, and I excuse the inexcusably stylistic only
as it is coincidentally true—the border guards, et cetera,
are looking not at a criminal but at one who has strived
to avoid becoming one.

We may take our American fascination with police as a
desperate need to reinforce or confirm the existence of
the superego (Eric Hoffer wrote that in countries where
there is freedom, everyone demands equality, which is to
say, control).

So, perhaps, my appearance to the police is not a side effect but a (whether or not subconsciously generated or contrived) pose—an appeal to those forces supposedly in control to allow me to demonstrate essential harmlessness.

The security expert Gavin de Becker wrote that, to the social outcast, it is sometimes better to be wanted by the police than not to be wanted at all.

I would like to get through life without disgracing myself.

Curiously, to the artist, this must mean not *subscribing to* the social contract but resisting it—saying, or being prepared to say, the unacceptable.

Success ratifies the iconoclast, and places him or her in the strange position of having been endorsed for being a detractor.

To have Been True to the Truth, as it were, and not only escaped censure but gained praise puts the artist in the position of the Gingerbread Boy.

But perceptions change. Neither the artist nor his audience sees the world in the same way after twenty years—the world itself is, of course, not the same.

It was comfortable to become comfortable with iconoclasm, with the flare of the border guard, and to work or posture to deserve that glare; and it's all very well, but it probably is not that pursuit which must be carried out in solitude and as an act of creation rather than reaction.

Jafsie was a shadow figure in the Lindbergh kidnapping. He volunteered to act as a go-between, and may, in fact, have been part of the crime.

John Henry fought the steam drill through the moun-

tain, and, through that his momentary victory, established something other than the extent of his pride.

Perhaps Jafsie was a criminal, and perhaps John Henry
was a fool.

I offer these essays as examples of my search for a new
model.

David Mamet

tain, and, through that his momentary victory, established something other than the extent of his pride.

Perhaps Jafsie was a criminal, and perhaps John Henry was a fool.

I offer these essays as examples of my search for a new model.

David Mamet

Looking at Fifty

I have a list of challenges-for-cause through which I choose the films I watch.

Any film containing any of the disqualificatory elements listed below loses, at the point the enormity makes itself apparent, any further claim on me:

Any use of Handel's *Messiah,* or *The Four Seasons,* or Pachelbel's *Canon;* any slow-motion sequence of lovers out of doors; any rack-focus from grass, wheat, or other vegetables to a distant object; a list of seven or more persons whose title contains the word "producer" in any form; any shot of the protagonist twirling slowly with arms spread; a title card reading, "based on a true story"; and that, to me, unfailing diagnostic tool, a present participle in the title.

Now, why this sudden rush of wings? My theory is this: the present participle denotes an ongoing process. The dramatic form demands a process with a distinct beginning and end.

In the getting, looking at, going to films we are brought into a process of long duration, a "state," in effect, which will alter, if at all, only marginally by the end of the film.

Yes, we are uncaring, but we can be a little less uncaring; yes, we have difficulty "communicating," but perhaps there is some hope; yes, men and women are different, but, perhaps, in our very differences, et cetera. I'd rather watch birds molt.

And yes, *grossièreté maudite*, I have headlined this bumf "Looking at Fifty."

My excuse is that I am looking at fifty.

When young, history seems to us (1) Yesterday, (2) The Dinosaurs. As we approach our allotted span, history falls in upon itself like those Black Holes so beloved of *The New York Times*—a century, which is to the adolescent unimaginable eons, seems just within our grasp (I once had a cup of coffee with a fellow cabdriver who, when young, had driven for Robert Todd Lincoln).

One sees that human nature is unchanging, ever-bad, and that, like one's fellows, one is privileged to partake of the worst of it. And while our nature and disposition remains loathsome, cruel, and, at its best, pathetic, material circumstances, over one's lifetime, conspire to elaborate, degenerate, and thus rob life of those last remaining purities undebauched by progress.

We see that Yesterday and Today, the Angry Young Man and the Old Fart, are one. The astounding breakthrough is, time after time and yet again, revealed as the scourge of humankind, and "that's how it is on this bitch of an earth"—

the process of history is ongoing, unchanging save for lesser or greater novelties of folly. It will end much as it began and no one the better for it.

Yes, yes, as at the Bad Film, this or that one, at the deathbed or at the bier, will say, "What a difference," "What a noble mind is here o'erthrown," or "What a loss to the automotive sales community," and the wheel grinds on.

I am sick of being young. I haven't been young for years.

I *am*, like Maurice Chevalier, "glad I'm not young anymore," and I wish I'd just turn fifty and be done with it.

I've been, for years, while considering myself the Kid, the oldest person in the rehearsal room, on the film set, et cetera, and only seem to run into my elders with any regularity at the odd laudatory dinner, at many of which I find myself speaking, and what must *that* portend if not that soon I shall, if God sees fit to spare me, find myself in the even less supportable position of being honored—listening to the speaker while trying to compose the features into that attitude conglomerated of humility, interest, retrospection, and gratitude, the difficult production of which is so like the actions of the vaudeville spinner-of-plates-upon-sticks.

The very title of this essay is proof positive of my failing powers—powers no longer sufficient to create, sufficient only to thank those whose praise of a life-well-spent, of lifetime achievement, et cetera, must and can only mean they wish one's death. Ingrates. And have they never read *King Lear*, and are they, then, incapable of education, wisdom, of true gratitude, of, in short, reverence for their elders?

The Stoic wrote: you will not have to face Old Age; that man is being trained now, by the gods. And it must be so.

The Older Woman dons excessive wrist jewelry and over-
size eyeglasses, the winded writer takes up the political,
the depraved discover God, and history continues not
only to implode but to accelerate its implosion insup-
portably.

But, nay, time, like pain, cannot be both unbearable and
interminable—save, of course, at a French movie, which
is the challenge-for-cause I forgot to include in the opening, and thank you for your time.

Five-Mile Walk

There was nothing to do.

We'd throw the ball up onto the garage roof in the evenings, but we never would during the day.

It was an excellent game. The one would put the beach ball up onto the low-pitched roof, and put a secret spin on it. The other would have to divine where it would come off of the roof, and catch it before it hit the ground.

Or we could walk the half-mile to the basketball half-court, but we were small, and the hoop was so high, and none of us were good at the game.

So we would play "horse." I had the two shots: the one, to bounce the ball into the basket; the other, to stand on the free-throw line, my back to the hoop, and heave the ball over my head.

Or we could walk and talk, and discuss topics of which

I remember only the one: Sue Ann, and whether and how often she had gone all the way and with whom.

Or we could take the five-mile walk down to the ice-cream stand on U.S. 30, which is the Lincoln Highway.

It begins in Boston and runs west to James Fraser's statue *End of the Trail* in California. It appears in Woody Guthrie's song "Hard Traveling" ("I've been hitting that Lincoln Highway/I thought you knowed . . ."), and it appeared in a linguistics seminar as the "greasy/greazy line," that delineator of North-South differences in pronunciation. More enterprising youths, blasted by the burden of a suburban summer, might have dreamt of following it west.

We could not say we hiked down to the highway; we dragged ourselves those dead five miles. We got our ice-cream cone, and dragged ourselves those five miles back to sit out the midwestern afternoon and wait for dusk. At dusk we would play ball-on-the-roof, or Peggy-move-up, or horse, or twenty-one. We would walk to the golf course, and burrow under the fence and steal the flags.

Now and then we would take the train into the City. We were interested in climbing and trespassing.

We would climb the girders of a bridge. We would break into a building under construction, and explore. We went to the Museum, and spent a day walking the pediments, among the caryatids, thirty feet off the ground.

When I was by myself I would spend the day in the city shoplifting.

Or I would haunt the library. I'd walk the stacks—the floor was made of glass bricks, and they fascinated me. I'd find a likely-looking novel and read it in the big room, and find

another, and read that, until it was time to return home.
And as an older adolescent, living in the city, I would dress
in a sport coat and tie, evenings, and walk down to the ho-
tels, and find myself an empty ballroom, and sit in the dark
playing the piano.

Once I was whisked into the lake by a wave. And once I
spent a night and a morning on the beach sick, drugged,
and hallucinating.

Once I spun a car out of control, one winter night, and
almost killed myself and the girl we thought I'd gotten
pregnant, at the end of the trip looking for an abortionist.

I saw tornadoes in the city, and the wet blood of a fourth-
grade friend in the alley where the car ran him down.

I used to lie on the eighteenth-story parapet of an apartment building, and will myself to sleep thinking, Should
I roll the one way I will die, the other way, I'll live.

I remember the passenger trains of the Illinois Central,
four blocks from my house in the evenings, and the slow
freights in the middle of the night, and may or may not
have thought that a more enterprising child might dream
of taking those trains south.

I remember courting girls in Hyde Park, and the interminable wait on the platform at one, two, three o'clock for
the train to take me home. And it seems I carved my initials
and those of one of the girls into a bench at a station, the
name of which is just beyond me.

I broke my nose playing football, I went to a Central
High school, and to the Bijou Theater, but none of it ever
seemed other than odd to me.

Salad Days

Thirty years ago I'd go to the Waverly Theater in the afternoon with a large cup of coffee with a little milk in it and a pack of Camels and I'd skip acting school to watch a double feature and come out only to go to work in the evening. I worked as an usher, then house manager, then assistant stage manager for *The Fantasticks*.

After work I would walk home the seventy or so blocks across upper Sixth Avenue and across the corner of the park to Seventy-first Street and Columbus.

On the weekends the fellows in the show would take me out for brunch at the Pam Pam on Seventh Avenue, or between shows on Sunday for a drink, a Bloody Mary or two, at Asher's on Christopher Street, and I suppose they were trying to court me, though I must have seemed to them a rather unformed thing, but perhaps that was the point.

My roommate at that time was studying dance at Juilliard,

and he kept bringing home perfect sixteen-year-old ballerinas. He got the bedroom and I got the couch in the living room. One night long, tall Jenny Hobs stopped by at eleven o'clock and flung a cat in the door and said, "He's yours. His name is Leonard." I kept him a short and difficult while and finally ditched him somewhere.

One night I woke up at four to hear that they had shot Bobby Kennedy on the radio I'd left on all night. I must have fallen asleep to the radio. I was fairly lonely in those days. One night in the middle of the night I was listening to the WMCA Good Guy Sweatshirt Offering on some call-in program and they asked the name of the pretty French girl on the Garry Moore show and I knew it was Denise Lor and I called in and said so and a month later there was a sweatshirt stuffed into my mail box and I was overcome by its compressibility.

Across the hall lived two exceptional young women, both small and beautiful. One was muscled and she was a flier in the circus and the other delicate and Irish and I longed for her through a very lonely year and at the end of which and upon my exit I discovered she'd had a similar pash for me. I moved out as I'd gotten a job in summer stock out on the tip of Long Island, and it may have been the only time, or at least one of the few times, I was ever hired as an actor. And then I left Seventy-first Street.

I remember food being very important up there. Days I would exist on a bowl of rice and beans which came with a small basket of bread. And when I was more flush I'd get a cup of café au lait and the occasionally prized Maduros Fritos. And weekends I lived on a quart of milk and a package of Milano cookies.

How I envied those glimpsed from afar who had, it seemed, their society intact, their support intact, their prospects and their careers before them. I moved in a daze. I was happiest on the walk up Sixth Avenue. What did I think of? Fame, success, love, being accepted. I ran into the cop and the kids having a snowball fight at midnight in Washington Square, New Year's Eve, 1967.

And I remember one of the players in *The Fantasticks* and I went out for a drink one night on Bleecker Street and he bought me a Margarita and he told me he wanted me to remember that it was he who bought me my first one and I do remember.

I remember afternoons at the Café Figaro, and the jazz at the Top of the Gate, and Kenny Rankin at the Bitter End and Steve Martin at the Bitter End and running the old complicated cross fade at the end of *The Fantasticks* on the rheumatic rheostat stick board in the lighting booth at the show and plunging everyone into darkness.

Someone wrote, as I read long ago, that artists moved to Greenwich Village in the twenties because the streets were short and winding and the bill collector had a difficult time finding his way.

It occurred to me years later that that was nonsense and that no one is more persistent than a bill collector. That they're infinitely more persistent than artists and that the artists must have come into the Village for another reason. Perhaps they came for love, for good coffee, and for the influx and availability of adventure-minded youth, and the permitted wistfulness of the whole damn thing.

If I could go back would I do it differently? Well, I can't go back.

And I remember Thompson Street in bed with a lovely young woman asleep and we'd let the candle burn down too low and I woke up and the walls and the Indian bedspread on the walls and the mattress were in flame and we were out on the street naked and shivering and I can't recall what happened next.

I remember my father coming down to visit me once or twice and going to hear jazz with him at the Top of the Gate after my show. Some of the fine times I remember that we had together.

And I remember envying those who took life easy, who were happy in love, who were happy in their work, with themselves, with their life.

If I could go back would I do it differently? Well, as I said, I can't go back. The altimeter seems to unwind and my past life and the remainder of my life rush before my eyes and I have become one of the fellows it seems I looked at longingly when I was a youth and there you have it.

Black Cashmere Sweater

My ten-year-old black cashmere turtleneck is old again. In each succeeding generation it seems to age more quickly.

My wife has worn mine over the years, and I remember the sweater coming off, drawn off over her head in that pose, like Picasso's sketch of the nursing mother, which is the quintessence of the feminine.

And I remember her rendition, her gift to me, which we called the Homeland Sweater after some romantic quote which most probably came from Hemingway.

I remember one of our too-many airports, and clasping her to me when she wore that sweater, and the press of travelers breaking around us, and then she got on the plane.

I remember her wearing it one freezing March night on the Vineyard, at some posh restaurant. The restaurant was deserted except for the middle-aged fellow and his wife across the room. They were involved in some misery compounded of fate and their own device, and we two were dopey in love, and she had on the black sweater, and looked like the Girl at the Half-Door, and that fellow looked at us with a longing that was like a knife in his gut.

I wore the sweater on those many transatlantic courting excursions.

Quite the perfect thing for the cold middle of the night.

I say the perfect thing, light and warm.

My friend B. sported a muffler-shawl last year, and asked me to feel it and tell me what the material was. Cashmere, of course, I said.

She shook her head. "It's from zee leetle hair from zee zroat of zee goat," she corrected, and indicated that this held trump over cashmere, but I can go nowhere near that far.

We read of cashmere in the Victorian novels as the stuff of the simple day-dress worn by the governess, and then it must have been, at least to the bourgeoisie, an everyday affair, chosen for warmth and durability.

But to me it has always been special.

In addition to its connection to courting, I associate it with the equally romantic directing-of-film.

There one would find oneself, togged out for night shooting, stomping around to keep warm on some deserted city street at four A.M.

All of the gawkers have slunk home, and there we are, making our movie in the dark and cold. Perfection. One of the layers in my necessarily layered look is the said black turtleneck. Other layers include a heavy hunting coat, labyrinthine with pockets original and aftermarket.

I found the coat in my closet, where it had hidden since my last film. In one of the pockets was a thumb-sized piece of red Korean ginseng which sustained me through weeks of cold night shooting some years ago—the ginseng another bit of high-ticket-yet-utilitarian perfection.

And the black turtleneck kept me warm as one of the layers of hunting garb in Texas, Maine, New Hampshire.

Perhaps it is not the best practice to wear the turtleneck as part of one's layering—the theory holds that layers should be capable of being opened or closed, to regulate the temperature—but my achilles' heel has always been my chest and throat. My body wants them covered, failing which it tends to break down. And in the aftermath I have used that black sweater as a sickroom garment, and have lain in bed shivering and gaunt and sweating into it in what I hope was an acceptable rendition of our homage to the Aesthete Tubercular of century just passed.

I know the moths do not actually eat the wool, that they lay their eggs, or some such, or so we are told—that the eggs do the damage.

But the moths have eaten my sweater, as they ate the last one, and the one before that, and that takes me back thirty years, to the beginning of my history with the garment.

Like the black beret (which one is always told is *blue*; but mine is black), the black cashmere turtleneck is a perfect garment (cf. Horst, Avedon, Irving Penn, et al.).

It accentuates the jawline, or, in its absence, suggests it, and, by extension, character.

It frames the face, it renders the torso more unitary and shapely, it warms, it can be worn casually or under the sport

coat or suit as the closest approximation to the required-but-absent shirt and tie, in that contest one will likely but not necessarily lose to the maître d'. (May I suggest: "What if I were to inform you I *have* on a shirt and tie, that they are covered by my sweater, which, for reasons of health, I am forbidden to remove?" I ask that the reader note that my setting the suggestion in a conditional clause might spare all but the most inveterate opponents of casuistry the egregious, demeaning, and unnecessary utterance of The Fib).

The black beret, the black turtleneck, and I am hard-pressed to think of the perfect third to round the company out.

In times of transient victory over my metabolism I have tucked the sweater into my jeans, cinched the belt tight, turned the tweed cap brim-to-the-back, and felt the complete Martin Eden.

Such an ensemble will either make one look good, or as good as one is ever going to look, and, therefore, make one feel good. No wonder I associate the sweater with love; it shares its job description.

Now, falling in love is our most beloved transition, and seems to occur during the transitional seasons.

Summer is the time for dalliance, and winter the time for comfort; but spring and, more particularly, fall are the time for love, and what better to wear and remember than that black cashmere turtleneck.

We were plagued in philosophy class by the question of the Hammer: The handle breaks and we replace the handle. Later the head breaks, and we replace the head. Is it now the same hammer?

The question of the Hammer could be argued yea or nay;

but the moths have eaten my black sweater, and when the new one comes out of the box it will be by acclimation, by courtesy, and in fact, my same black cashmere turtleneck.

So doth philosophy serve Humankind. *Shanti.*

Cops and Cars

Two stories, twenty years apart.

I was driving a cab. I'd stopped, over by Bughouse Square, to smoke a cigarette. I started to pull out, looked behind me, pulled out in traffic, and felt a jolt. I'd been hit by a cop car.

He got me quartering away.

The cop jumped out of his car, all solicitude.

"Jeez," he said, "are you okay? I wasn't looking. I took the corner too fast. Are you okay? I'm *sorry* . . ." and so on. I allowed I was fine, we looked at the two cars, him apologizing all the while. There was a dent in the rear wheel well of the cab, but it wasn't going to be noticed among the other nicks. And there was a dent in the cruiser's grille.

"Oh, jeez," he said, and shook his head. "I gotta report that. I got to fill out a report. Would you mind waiting? I've got to have my supervisor look at that."

I agreed to wait, and very soon *several* police vehicles

screamed up, and my statement was taken, and noted, and I was cited for reckless driving and damage to city property.

I had to go to Court, and it didn't look good at all.

It looked like a hefty fine and the suspension of my license, which I was using to drive the cab and make my living.

A friend of my dad's was a criminal lawyer, and he agreed to go with me to court. I asked when we could get together to go over the facts of the case. He said to meet him at Court on the Day.

He was, as is the way of lawyers, late, and we had no time to discuss the case at all. He charged into Court, with me behind him, begging for one moment to describe the events and the justice of the case. He shrugged me off. The clerk called the case and the lawyer strode to the front and said, "Your honor, what we have here is a young law student, top of his class at Northwestern University"—I couldn't *find* Northwestern University—"who is struggling to pay his tuition. When he isn't studying, he is driving his cab, and he cut it too thin, he was overtired, he wasn't paying attention, he is extraordinarily sorry, and anything your honor could do to . . ." Well, I got sentenced to remedial driver's education, four Tuesday nights, and my crime was as if it had never been. Next case.

Twenty years later and several blocks away, I was directing a film. We were due to shoot the morning scene on Oak Street beach and the afternoon scene on Elm Street.

But the wind was blowing high, and when we got on the beach at dawn, it was clear we couldn't shoot there till the wind went down.

Some clear head suggested we flip the schedule and

shoot the beach in the afternoon, and we trudged over to Elm Street.

The plan was good, but for the presence of the passenger cars on the street. We needed that room for our trailers and generator and camera trucks. The street had been posted for days with a sign which read, "Such-and-such-a-date, this street closed from (here, in a blank, was written NOON)— any cars found past this time will be towed."

So there we were. We needed to shoot, we needed the cars gone. Whatever could we do? "What a dilemma we are in," we said to each other.

The head of our police escort listened, as we wrung our hands, took out a magic marker, crossed out the word NOON where it appeared and wrote in DAWN, and towed the cars.

Six Hours of Perfect Poker

I think back and remember the fellow's fear as the missing term in a dream.

The fellow was a latecomer to a pot-limit Hold 'em game at a Lake Tahoe casino in the late eighties, and he sat down to a game I'd been bulling for an afternoon.

I was in Tahoe preparing a film, and found that this, like other periods of pre-production, was a heady time: I, director, dispensed patronage and made decisions whose worth would not be tested for some weeks but whose existence was applauded and endorsed by friends and co-workers alike. I was sitting on top of the world.

So I thought I'd play poker.

I was a twenty-year member of a vicious home game up in Vermont.

Our game was Hold 'em, and we played pot-limit, just as they did at the casino.

I'd been playing it for twenty years, here I was in Nevada, and it was time for me to sit down.

I prepared myself. I dressed in black, put on my sunglasses, had a good breakfast, and reviewed my tools.

My tools were, as I reviewed them, somewhere between meagre and fairly respectable: I knew the odds and percentages, I could manage money; I could, when required, control my love of action; finally—and I counted this above all—I had a very good sense-of-play, that is to say, a feeling for the table.

Such an instinct never served me in a limit game (that is, a game where there is a cap on the bets), but had, in the past, come in handy in pot-limit, where a player with a marginal hand or marginal confidence may be manipulated through the betting.

So I sat down, and neither joked nor smoked. I drank water, and kept myself physically still. I limited my speech to monosyllables, and I (perhaps not coincidentally) played better poker than I'd ever played in my life.

The men and women did indeed put their pants on one leg at a time, and common sense and aggression on my part were ruling the day. I bulled the game.

I played position better than I ever had, I stole the antes, I could not be caught, I played at the minimum-acceptable "third level," and did it effortlessly. (Maslansky and Sklar, in their *Hold 'em Poker* state categorically that the absolute minimum skill necessary to play in a professional game is ability to think at the third level. Level One: What does he have? Two: What does he think I have? Three: What does he think I think *he* has?)

Being of an undisciplined frame of mind, I found and find

it difficult to formulate such strict constructions, and in my cardplaying career tend to rely more often on the less taxing (and less rewarding) "I've got a feeling." But *that* day the third level was clear to me. And, *as* importantly, I played a game sufficiently aggressive to deprive the other players of the chance to employ their (undoubtedly possessed) cognitive skills greater than mine. (They could not remember to drain the swamp, as I was the coterie of alligators.)

Some fellow who, like me, came from one of those states which begin with a vowel, and he came to New York in the 1920s, and wrote home, "No one knows me here. No one will know or care what I do or whether I live or die. No one knows who I am. What bliss."

That's how I felt at that poker game. I had re-invented myself. Hell, I had *invented* myself. The first thirty-some years had been an accretion of mischance and necessity. I was now doing the job right.

Who is that fellow in the dark glasses? Answer: none of your business; bet, check, or fold.

It was blatant, and it was damned enjoyable. Looking back, I see that I made the table respect me as I operated in a manner worthy of respect—I pushed the pushable positions, I avoided the questionable ones, and if they did not know I was playing above my head, that was worthy of respect, too.

I made them play a vanilla game, as that was the game I could win; and, as the afternoon wore on, I made a lot of money doing it.

The feeling was magnificently unequivocal.

Is this a particularly masculine enjoyment? I don't know.

A lot of drivel has been written in our lifetime about the word "macho"; which word seems to mean not only "male and degenerate-ludicrous" but "male and therefore degenerate and ludicrous."

I was passing a food shop in Cambridge, Mass., one day, and stopped to wonder at a series of T-shirts and bumper stickers in the window, all of which derogated men.

I was about to shrug and walk on, when I reflected that such divisiveness and confrontationalism wasn't very nice and, more to the point, that I didn't like it.

I went in and spoke to a clerk. "Excuse me," I said. "You have material in the window mocking men. If you were to remove the word 'men' from your bumper stickers and replace it with, for example, some racial designation, I think you would see that the materials in question are in rather poor taste." "Well, I don't know," he said, "we sell a lot of 'em!"

So: to hit the target, to bring home the money, to put the other fellow on the mat, will I fall into the solecism of the food store clerk and first denominate these enjoyments as male and then use the fact of the denomination to question their legitimacy?

Will I go so far as to suggest that in a country and a time where the traditionally male model of breadwinner is less possible of accomplishment, the epithet "macho" is employed, finally, not as an indictment of possession of supposedly male attributes but as an indictment of their relative absence?

In any case, it is possible that this love of the unequivocal, of that victory not necessitating interpretation, is a survival of the Chase, and who is to say?

But I will say it is sweet.

And it was sweet for six hours, until I "came to" in the coffee shop of the hotel.

A fellow player sat down next to me. "My name is James," he said. I nodded.

"What happened?" he said.

What happened is this: it got on toward dinnertime, and I was still the boss hog.

I got Jack-Queen in the hole. I'm bulling the game. I'm down in third position, checked to me, I bet. Now fellow, sitting behind me, calls, three more call. One raises. I raise back, everyone stays on one. But the flop comes, Jack-Queen-four. Two hearts.

I have the two top pair. Checked to me, I bet. I have the two top pair, nobody's raised me; new guy after me raises, others fold, and I raise him back: what could he have? He could have, *significantly,* a set (trip) Jacks or Queens. And that would be consistent with his play before the flop. Let's see. I raise him back, he only calls. Fine. I was good indeed.

Fourth Streets falls a ten, no heart. I bet, new guy calls. Only calls. Fine. Comes the river, falls a four; again, no heart.

Now, I've got the two top pair. If he'd had a set, now he'd have a boat, but I could not put him on the set, there is no flush. I think back, it occurs to me, I've got to win. I've got to hold the winner. I *have* him.

There are some considerable thousands of dollars in the pot. I look across at the man. He's sitting there sweating.

What does it mean? Obviously, he's afraid.

Well, I think, let's see what he'll *stay* for, and I make a *moderate* bet. And he calls, we turn over our hands, I say,

"Two top pair," and he says, "Straight," and turns over the nine-King, of hearts. "Straight? *What* straight . . . ?" I say.

But, of course, there it is.

You poker players read along, and you said, of my record of the hand, "The fellow has a *straight*. What *else* would he be staying with?"

You may remember in grade school the demonstration of the blind spot in the eye: the optic nerve connects to the back of the eye, and at the point of its connection we are blind. We cannot see what's there. You place the eraser on the table, and move it away from you and at a certain point it disappears.

I could not see that straight.

In retrospect it is *blatant*. I had to put him on *either* trip Jacks, trip Queens (he would not have stayed prior to the flop with a pair of fours), Ace-Jack, Ace-Queen, or some possible flush-or-straight draw.

He'd played before the flop with the nine-King suited, the flop hit, he was sitting with four hearts to the King flush, and a gut-straight, the ten hits on the turn, and he's got the boss straight.

Ten years later I still hear myself saying, "What straight?" and the mighty were fallen.

What an unsatisfactory end to a good afternoon. I got up from the table a loser, and found myself in the coffee shop.

"What happened?" James said. "We were watching you, we all wondered, 'Who is this guy?'" And then he said, "You just played six hours of perfect poker."

What an acknowledgment. I sat down with the pros and won, and then gave it all back not through an error in

judgment or character, not through avarice or folly, not, finally, through any of the manifold historic ways the poker
player knows to betray himself and his best interests, but,
it seemed, through a totally new one: I went blind on a
hand.

Did I do it to punish myself? That is, of course, the question with which I plagued myself. I cannot say that I feel
that was my desire, but there are the facts.

One could assert that I must have been acting to punish
myself, for that is what occurred; any nonemotional analysis would have to so conclude.

Like many gamblers, and, perhaps, like all gamblers at
some time, I have punished myself, and I am too well
aware what that feels like; and this did not feel like that.

The answer to "What happened?" was, and is, "I just don't
know."

But recently I had a clue.

It is my experience in the analysis of dreams, as in the
construction of Drama (which is nothing other than an inversion of the process), that it is invariably the overlooked,
the seemingly innocuous, the dismissed "connective" term,
which is the clue to the mystery.

In *Oedipus* it is the dismissed lowly shepherd, the "worthless" man, who must explain life to the King.

In this poker dream or drama I think it is the fellow's fear.
For ten years I wondered why I did not see the straight. Recently I began to wonder why I did not see his fear.

He was apprehensive when he sat down (I had been
bruited as a formidable player), and he negotiated the hand
with a certain diffidence, which evaporated when the ten
fell; but HE WAS FRIGHTENED AT THE END, WHEN THE FOUR PAIRED.

I, in my "blindness," overlooked not only the tale of the cards but the tale of the fellow's demeanor.

I chose to interpret his tremor as a knowledge of the weakness of his hand, and so I bet-out moderately, and he stayed for the bet.

But why? Such play on my part was amateurish. What could he beat? What had he *stayed* on?

The four could not *conceivably* aid him. It was not a heart, I'd discounted any possibility of trips, he had to've been beaten, and *know* himself beaten (as I figured it), and why would he, then, stay for *any* bet? Thinking back, I seem to remember some dim consciousness of betting small out of fear of the full house (the now-paired fours on the board could give him a full house); and there is the clue. My memory of fear is not, finally, of his but of my *own*: I feared the full house.

Why? He could not, again, have the full house without previously having had trips (I could not put him on four-Jack, four-Queen, or four-nine), so what was I afraid of?

Even had I *seen* the straight, and correctly read him for it, my move, at that time, was to *bet-out heavily*, and make him wonder if *I* had the full house (with which every move of mine was consonant); but, no, I did the one thing which would give him the pot, I made it cheap to get in—I abdicated, in effect, what was the power position *even in the absence of the winning hand*, and left the game a loser.

Of *course* I was punishing myself. How can I think otherwise?

What could be better than six hours of perfect poker, what less equivocal, what more enjoyable to contemplate?

I went on to direct the movie. I played a few times during the filming, and lost consistently.

On coming home I found that it was gone. I didn't want to play anymore. I woke up one day and it was gone. I'd heard the older fellows, avid hunters, talk about it: "One day I just didn't want to hurt anymore—one day I woke up, and it was gone." "Why?" "I don't know, it was just gone."

And how it happened to me. I was changed.

The desire to play poker—sometimes a mania, always an excitement—which I'd had for twenty-some years, was just gone, and I didn't miss it.

I would like to look back to that hand and say that it was not the cause but simply the announcement of the change.

That would be a dignified and diplomatic rendering of the facts. I will extend myself the courtesy.

Scotch Malt Whisky Society

I'd had my heart broken and was looking for help.

I called a fellow I knew and asked if I could come by. He said yes, and we talked all night, and drank two and a half fifths of Bell's scotch while doing it.

The sun rose and I felt comforted and wise for about a block of the walk home, and then I didn't taste scotch for twenty years.

Fade out, fade in. Again, it occurs to me, I was being comforted for some enormity my endocrine system had involved me in. I was sitting in a bar in Cambridge, Mass.

My friend said to the bartender, "Give 'im a shot of your best whisky."

The bartender reached down a bottle from the top shelf.

"That's the ticket," my friend said. "What is it?"

The bartender said some foreign name.

"Fine," my friend said, "how much?" Sixty-four dollars, he was told.

"Expensive bottle," he said.

"No," he was corrected, "by the shot."

"Put it back," my friend said. "He's not that unhappy. Give 'im something in the ten-buck range." And the bartender poured me a shot of an ambrosia which I only afterward discovered to be scotch.

I drank it.

"Well, hell," I said, "this puts any cognac in the shade." The bartender nodded.

I remember riding in the car with my dad in the fifties, him driving and smoking a Lucky.

On the pack it said, "It's toasted!" And that's how they smelled to me.

The cigarettes smelled like the toasted almonds on the Toasted Almond Good Humor bar, which is to say, perfect; and my years of smoking were an addiction both to the nicotine and to the notion that the next one might just taste like they smelled when my dad was driving the car.

Similarly with alcohol, much of my—and perhaps your—drinking was a search for that magical indulgence with which the grown-ups seemed so pleased.

The cognacs were, to me, too sweet, as were even the sharpest bourbons.

Scotch was, in my experience, a thin, acid poison.

I drank when I was young because I was young, for all those pleasant reasons, one of which was an aid to my choking down the cigarette smoke.

I held the midwestern belief that anyone who knew too much about wine would do well to guard that knowledge closely, that cognac was just sweet rye, and that opera was just fat ladies shrieking. (I recognized and relaxed in the very similar proletarian disposition/pretension of Edinburgh and Glasgow, where one could, I was told, drive a Bentley but would have to explain it as a *"Workingman's Bentley."*)

Yes, Scotland, I say. And there I was at the bar in Cambridge, Mass., that charming Athena of Backwaters, and I tasted the good scotch and thought, "How long has this been going on?"

It tasted like it might have tasted in a world where all advertisements were not only true but brought to our attention to increase our happiness.

It was dark and rich and not at all sweet, and quite sharp without being bitter, and it tasted overridingly of smoke and, curiously, of iodine. It didn't taste like any scotch I'd drunk or could imagine. (I try to think of things as perfect-of-their-kind, and comes to mind only the I.B.M. Selectric typewriter and the mid-sixties Karmann Ghia. If I can get giddy about them, I suppose I can get giddy about scotch. In for a penny, et cetera.)

Which brings me to Edinburgh.

It is, I think, equal to Jerusalem in beauty. The Castle's up there on the black lava rock, like an adolescent girl's fantasy. The whole city's gray stone, and it rains and is cold all the time, and that's just fine. Maugham wrote there are climates where one writes and climates where one sweats, and I vote with him.

I asked my wife why I saw such a lot of old people walking around Edinburgh, and she said, "It's healthy. And the people enjoy themselves."

I think that much of our American attitude toward pleasure can be seen in the coy, childlike behavior of the flight attendant offering a dessert:

"Are you sure that I can't tempt you . . . ?"

"Thank you, no."

"Just a liiiiiittle bit . . . ?"

Well, no, you know, it's an ice-cream sundae. I haven't had one in thirty years, and if I did require one, I would not need the accompanying nursery charade.

"Are you sure that I can't tempt you to this naughty pleasure?"

Our undeniable Puritan society can countenance chastity or pornography, but little in between. It seems we have a problem with the issue of control, and that we cycle from conservative to liberal excesses like a child with two sets of toys—joy with the new giving way to boredom, at which point the old is produced to our amnesiac delight.

It is an atmosphere productive of pleased tattletales and uneasy libertines, a Puritan country, in short.

No, but I gotta say . . .

(I take the above from *il miglior fabbro,* Alan King, who, years ago, solved the problem of the segue beautifully, elegantly, and categorically. He tells the joke, adjusts his tie, and says, "No, but I gotta say," and proceeds to a completely unrelated matter.)

Now this:

We were in Edinburgh visiting the in-laws. I was, as usual, being a grumpy old curmudgeon. My people don't travel well. For the past six thousand years we usually moved only because someone was trying to kill us.

That is my excuse, and I am not too proud to use it, and am happy to share it with you.

So there I was, jet-lagged and grumpy in Edinburgh.

"How would you like to visit the Scotch Malt Whisky Society?" Trevor asked.

"Okay," I said.

We went down to Leith, the old port of Edinburgh, to the Vaults, which claims to be the oldest building in continuous commercial use in Britain—built in the fourteenth century and, for some hundreds of years, a storage and auction house for sherries and other wines from the South. The sherry arrived, was auctioned and bottled, and the casks were bought up by the Scots, who aged their whisky in it.

So the whisky, the true Scotch single-malt, gets much of its flavor and all of its color from the cask. It can be aged in casks once holding sherry, or bourbon, or casks previously unfilled, and its character will, in the main, come from the wood, its previous contents, the age and history of the cask; a second-fill cask will have a different character than a first-fill.

The character of the whisky will also come from the water, the position in the "run," as the whisky is drawn from the still, the nature of the malt, the time in the cask, and, I am told, even the position of the cask in the maturing room—a more moist corner imparting a deeper flavor.

The basic ingredients and the basic technique, like acting, cooking, courting, and the other fine arts, are simple and straightforward. Barley is soaked and the grains allowed to germinate. It is dried in a kiln—by peat smoke, in the best breweries. The malted barley is dressed (cleansed of sprouts and imperfections), ground, and mashed with hot water. The liquid is extracted several times at increasing heats. The final liquid is called "wort." Yeast is added to the wort, and the mixture is distilled—boiled into vapor and chilled back into liquid—several times. The final distillate is Scotch whisky, which is aged in casks, bottled, sold, and drunk.

(I am indebted to David Daiches, and his most clear, charming and informative *Scotch Whisky: Its Past and Present* for the above rendition of the distilling process.)

So down, I say, I went to Leith, and there met Pip Hills, head of the Society.

Pip is a Scotsman, a lover, protector, and practitioner of true Scottish culture.

Mark Twain wrote that *Ivanhoe* was the book that ruined the South.

And there is, I think, a certain addictive similarity of wistfulness in the two conquered countries. (Not too very long ago the British postal system designated Scotland N.B., i.e., North Britain.)

In the late seventies Pip and some friends would tour the small distilleries and purchase for themselves a cask or so of the true native potation. This was (and is) the true single-malt, straight from the still to the cask, nondiluted and unfiltered. The scotch sold in the U.S. as a single-malt is approximately 50 percent of cask strength and has been filtered to remove undissolved solids.

England discovered scotch in 1890, when it replaced brandy as their national drink. Its discovery came about as part of their apostrophization of Scottish culture. The Victorian English made a fetish of Scotland, and frolicked in its kilts and tartans, and Scotland changed, in their estimation, from a backwater to a wild and romantic, more "natural" spot. Well, the designation "tourist attraction" tends to adulterate and eventually to obliterate the local character. Montana becomes Mount Rushmore, the quaint fishing village becomes Cannes—or Provincetown—and Scotland, a vassal state of England, became Scotland-land. Scotch replaced brandy, and a way was found to make it faster, cheaper, and worse.

The Patent Still substituted grain-neutral spirits for malted barley, blends replaced the single-malt, color was added; and scotch became England's and then the world's favorite drink.

Scotch whisky was a farm product, a cottage industry, an indigenous treasure, like maple syrup, or white lightning, full of character, idiosyncrasy, and taste; and now this thin, characterless blended drink was being sold under the same name and made me ill in 1967.

Pip Hills and his friends decried this "tartanry," they toured the distilleries to buy the odd cask first for their own consumption, and, one thing led to another, and in 1983 they founded the Scotch Malt Whisky Society in Leith, and there you are.

On my first visit Pip took me to the Members' Room, and took down ten bottles, and poured a thimbleful of each. The colors ranged from straw to lemon to red-brown. We tried the bouquet, first without and then with a bit of water—the water changed each bouquet dramatically—and then had a small sip of each. The whiskys were listed on the bottle and the brochure by age, cask number, region, and characteristics, but never by the name of the distillery. For example: "Highland Northern: like tooth-tincture in honey. Distilled, April, '76. Gold with a touch of green. Bourbon cask. Nose rich and creamy, of cut grass and malt to begin, of oil and cloves with water. Taste very sweet, wild and astonishing. Medicinal but not peaty . . ." (Sound good?)

Well, they all sounded good, and they all tasted good. The ten were extraordinarily various. I tasted each, and my easily identifiable favorite was that Lagavulin, potation of the gods, which I'd first encountered in the bar at Cambridge.

I spent a lovely afternoon at the Society, resisted buying one of their ties, and went off with a cask-strength bottle and their brochure. I got a kick out of that brochure. These fellows enjoyed writing about whisky. I found whisky described as peppery, woody, tasting of vanilla, of straw, of leather, of apricots, of nutmeg, wet hay, creosote, saddle soap, rhubarb—and I remembered tasting the whiskys and thinking, "Yes, it's true, it's that various." And I wondered who arrived at these distinctions.

What immortal hand or eye was framing these luscious descriptions? What agency was raising the status of what could arguably be described as mere booze to that of Art?

On my next trip to Edinburgh I got to find out.

We were once again visiting the Old Folks at Home; and I, as usual, arrived jet-lagged, and happily out-of-sorts.

I announced I was going to bed, and would see everyone the following noon. Would I not like to stay up for supper? No, no, thank you, I said, much too fatigued.

The phone rang, and it was Pip Hills. They were having a tasting, he said, a meeting of the few cognoscenti who chose and then described the whiskys which would be offered to the Society. Would I like to come?

Yes. I would. Well, the meeting was to be in Leith in one hour. I will now confess.

Once, on a trip to the previously mentioned Jerusalem (no, but I gotta say ...) I was invited to study Torah with a world-renowned scholar. My wife and I were both acquainted with his works, and excited at the prospect. Then we were informed/reminded that his particular profession of faith did not admit women to study. So we, regretfully, declined.

You see where this story is going.

Yes, Pip, I said, I would love to come to the tasting, and might it, do you think, be inappropriate if I were to bring my wife?

He said he did not think it was particularly the thing, and I found myself in the position of wondering if I were the sort of man who would decline the possibility of religious enlightenment which did not include my wife but would accept a similarly exclusive invitation to taste whisky.

Yes, I was that kind of guy. "Darling," I said, "I'm off to Leith. Do not wait up."

I adore Scotland. One afternoon I was haunting the Botanics—the Royal Botanical Gardens, Edinburgh, which manages to be a surpassingly lovely spot despite being filled with what can only be described as "plants"—I was in the checkout line at the café up at the top, and I was looking out of the windows at a faraway cathedral and, beyond it, the Pentland Hills.

I'd been to a wedding the day before at Rosslyn Chapel out by or perhaps in those very hills. Many of the men wore kilts.

A fellow told me afterward that Rosslyn Chapel is the spot most sacred to world Free Masonry. He told me that the Holy Grail is buried at Rosslyn Chapel, that the intricate stone carvings around the doors are sacred to the

Devil, and that they depict intricacies of a religion far pre-dating Christianity.

He took me back inside the Chapel and showed me the "Apprentice Column." It is an extraordinarily intricate—and nonetheless beautiful—piece of stone carving, a column up by the altar.

The other columns in the group are fairly plain, and this one stands idiosyncratically turned and worked, disbalancing, but, if I may, giving a rather lovely weight to the whole effect.

An apprentice, the man told me, was assigned the work of this one column.

When the master mason saw the beauty of the work, he ordered the apprentice killed.

He may have added that the apprentice himself was buried in the Chapel, but if he did I chose and choose to ignore it, as that would tend to take his two disparate and intriguing tales and suggest a unifying *idée fixe* bordering on the unfortunate.

Rosslyn Chapel is gorgeous. It is small and cold and carved everywhere.

I shuddered at the geometry—or perhaps it is trigonometry—necessary to align those stones. I thought of the old saw that the cathedrals took centuries to build, and yet no one's name is found on them.

Is it my imagination, I wondered, or is this story always and only repeated by those with a second-class mind?

So I mused in the checkout line, and the pretty young girl at the cash register said, "Fritz Kahn."

Fritz Kahn, I thought. Yes. Architect. No. If it's an architect it's Louis Kahn. Or Robert Kahn ...

"Fritz Kahn?" she said.

I nodded, playing for time. Surely, though, there *is* an architect of that name. But how did she know the tend of my thoughts?

"Fritz *Kahn*, sir . . . ?" she said.

"I'm sorry," I said. "Could could could, could you repeat that slowly?"

"D' you want a Fritz Kahn?" she said, and pointed down at some pastries a sign proclaimed to be the day's special: fruit scone.

And *yet* I maintain there is, or should be, an architect of that name.

And I also had a marvelous morning at a café called the Something-or-other, up by the castle. I sat at a table on the second floor, with an oblique view down the town and all the way to Fife, drinking basins of coffee and stuffing myself with breads, writing intently and watching various squads of young folks courting.

The young people seem happier in Edinburgh, too. Alright, I am a sucker for things Scottish—Jean Redpath, James Bond's housekeeper, my wife.

Ah, yes. I'm off to Leith, I said.

We met in the small boardroom of the Vaults. On one wall there was a low niche, from the floor to, perhaps, five feet in height.

On my first visit Pip asked me to guess its purpose.

Statuary came to mind but was not interesting enough for me to employ it as one of my guesses. "Don't know," I said. Closest thing, it resembles the niche in the "coffin corner" of a staircase.

Pip had never heard of that and so I accomplished my

objective of unseating him—for the nonce—as the master of mystery, and installing myself. But it seems the niche was the appointed station of the auctioneer in days gone by (you will remember the Vaults was employed as a warehouse and auction house for sherry, as early as six hundred years ago).

Back then, it seems, the people were in fact quite small. That's where the auctioneer stood, and the prospective buyers took the rest of the room to make their assessments and bid on the goods.

No, but I gotta say, which was just the sort of clambake to which I'd been invited that night.

I showed up in a respectful coat and tie. The others were dressed variously—jeans and leather jackets, jeans and sport coat, two fellows in suits.

The tasters were men from mid-forty to mid-eighty. The youngest was a wine merchant, the eldest was David Daiches, author of the aforementioned *Scotch Whisky: Its Past and Present*; there were a physics professor, a commercial man, a barrister, a fellow who I think was ex-military, Pip, myself, a total of eight.

We began with a Portuguese wine brought by the wine merchant.

It was rather stunningly good and was called Quinta de la Rosa, 1992.

We had a cracker and some cheese, and then we sat down.

It was as good as a poker game.

We had eight whiskys to taste; we had eight glasses in front of us, a pitcher of water and another for spit.

Pip began. He'd announce the whisky's name (this information wouldn't appear on the Society's bottled offering to its members), and he would pass the bottle around. We'd each take perhaps a half-ounce, and would discuss it in this order: by color, by bouquet. By bouquet after the addition of water, by taste, by general impression.

We would then assign it a score from one to ten, ten being the best.

I was told that our sense of smell is vastly more perceptive than our sense of taste; that taste is, in fact, made up primarily of smell; that our perception of taste is basically limited to sweet, sour, salty, bitter, but our descriptions of smell are virtually limitless.

In gauging the bouquet the gents held their nose over the glass, swirled the liquor, as one would expect, and also rubbed it on the back of the hand (this was a test for "smoke," which would appear in the bouquet as the whisky evaporated), and rubbed it between their palms. Before the tasting began, Doogie—whose treatment by Pip seemed to indicate his place as somewhere between "factotum" and "brains of the outfit"—Doogie, I say, brought around a cookie tin filled with what appeared to be charred black cloths and corks.

Several of the men sniffed the contents.

It seems that at the last tasting someone had suggested that a scotch tasted slightly of "bung cloth," and another, to aid in his ability to identify same in future samples, asked for some bung cloth to be procured for examination.

(Bung cloth being, of course, that cloth—burlap, or "hessian"—placed over the bung, or "stopper," to insure a tighter fit into the bunghole.)

This bung-detritus was charred from the sediment in the cask. It smelled sharp, and rather pleasant. I took a bit of the cloth and rubbed it between my palms and sniffed them, electing this a reasonable occupation for one who had no idea what he was doing.

So we began.

Blank Blank Distillery.

Sixteen years old. Water brings out the pepper. Oakey. More Islay than Orkney.

Comments come from around the table. Yellow cast. Peat and fruit. Peachy. Peppery. David Daiches identifies it as from a fino sherry cask.

Addition of water dissipates its peatiness. Brings out a saltiness. Pear drops on top. Gotten more bland. Now peppery. Taste thins. Takes a lot of water. Rate it a four. General agreement. Send to Sheol.

Mr. Daiches' comment reminds me of a story Zino Davidoff tells in his fine *Connoisseur's Book of the Cigar*: Two Cubans came into his shop. One chose a cigar and offered it to his companion, who identified it not only by maker but by year of manufacture and then identified the wrapper, the binder, and the filler, three separate tobaccos of which the cigar was made. Davidoff confessed himself impressed, and lamented that with the emigration of the old cigar manufactories from Cuba, such expertise would exist no more. But I saw it around the table, and was impressed and delighted to be included.

Thorstein Veblen reminded us that any endeavor using a preponderance of jargon is largely make-believe. But the talk around the table was not jargon, it was that of dedicated amateurs speaking lovingly of the object of their admiration, and doing so in standard and quite charming speech. We heard the designations—late run, early run, second-fill—but, in the main, the talk ran to concrete attempts to describe the evanescent: orange peel, citrusy, marzipan sweetness, almost like anchovies, yeasty aftertaste. Very clean, good breakfast whisky, good aperitif . . .

There is a sign in the Members' Room that connoisseurship is the adversary of inebriation; and, indeed, one could not have encountered a more respectful attitude than one found in the room. The tasters were engaging in preserving and extending a beloved native heritage—the single-malt local product, its vagaries and quiddities, distillery, by year and by cask, was of as much moment to them as is wine to the chaps in Bordeaux. In the best Scots tradition, their expertise was not that of an elite but of the simple citizen's right to enjoy the good things naturally incident to the locale.

Well, I was glad to be there.

"Linseed oil."

"Rubber . . . ? Does the water bring out rubber . . . ?"

"Hessian?"

"Verbena" (all chuckle).

"Tight-ass" (corrected to "reticent").

a) "I find it muddy."

b) "You've been very fortunate in the mud you've tasted."

So it went around. Sooty. Wood shavings. Caramel, corrected to "burnt-toffee." Brackish. The kind of whisky a lady ought to carry in her handbag (this the most aggressive opprobrium of the evening). Musky. Bicycle seat (with attendant digression). Nutmeg. Custard-apple . . .

I noticed that many of the descriptions were terms from

childhood. Well, of course, the senses are sharper then. Life is, for the happy child, simpler, and the special treats, the special pleasures, are pleasures, indeed.

Much of the delightful seemliness of the tasting consisted in this: We were indulging ourselves in a pleasure legitimately attendant upon advancing age. (Does not Escoffier remind us that the gustatory pleasure will persist when all others are gone?)

Our next-to-last whisky was aged thirty years. I suggested it would likely be quite good, and was informed yes, it would, or quite vile. It was reddish-dark. We heard "elusive, intoxicating nose." "Got to be a refill cask—no wood in the nose." The table got quiet as the men sniffed it. "Good quality fresh root ginger," one said.

Water is added, we taste, conversation derails. "Cinnamon on top." Pause.

"Very noble," all agree. Pause. "Spices come through on the palate."

It is awarded an eight, highest mark of any of the whiskys we taste in two sessions.

We go reluctantly on to the last of the evening, which nobody likes. "Miles away from the bonfire," says one. "Sour plaster." Pause. "Sour plaster." It is given a wretched four, and that's it for the business of the evening, and we all return to the previous whisky (Inchgower, 1966).

I am invited back the following week.

We taste another thirty-year-old, doesn't age well.

"As you would expect of an old whisky, no individual odors coming off. This whisky is a perfect example of the workings of natural justice—only the wealthy and misled will pay sixty pounds a bottle for it."

That evening we also hear, "Like the sea breeze blowing over grass," and of a Bruichladdich, 1979, "Not just balance, but coexistence," and then, "The distillery just closed down. It's a fucking disgrace."

I remember a wonderful inn-restaurant in South Royalton, Vermont. The cooking was French and light, and the food was hot and clean, and just right. Ten years intervened, and I found myself back. The name was the same, but it'd changed hands, some consortium had got it.

"How's the food?" I said. "Still good?"

"Well," the fellow said, "it's a lot more consistent."

Aha. Gene Debs said that you can vote for freedom and you'll probably lose or you can vote for slavery and you'll certainly win.

And our particular time and clime values the idea of "winning" above all else.

The province of the proletariat, fresh, simple food and drink—the local bakery or brewery, the pot still, hand-pressed cider—is now only enjoyed by a few. The Bruichladdich distillery closed (1979, "Subtle, beautifully balanced whisky, a refined drink"), and the lesson of Babel we see all day every day is that when too many of us band together we must turn to mischief.

I wrote long ago that fashion is an attempt to co-opt tragedy. I look back at that jejune pronounciamento and wonder if in spite of its being dramatic it might not after all be true.

White America not only expresses but, to a large extent, defines itself through African-American music and Jewish films.

Victorian England was raised on Scott's Waverley novels;

but England could not "have" the dignity and tragedy of the Scottish defeat—they say a loser can't get enough to eat and a winner can't sleep—so the English took the tartan, and *Waverley*, and glorified their Scots regiments, and took up drinking scotch.

Pip Hills and I were sitting in his kitchen in the New Town, Edinburgh.

The kitchen was graced by a fire-engine red Aga cooker—that stove-oven-cooktop-heater, which is the best of things British.

We were drinking superb coffee and feeling expansive. We spoke of things which were perfect-of-their-kind—the Aga, of course; I mentioned Lagavulin; the eighty-eight-inch wheelbase Land Rover; the old Rolex Explorer. He asked would I like to see the most beautiful object he had ever seen.

He brought out what looked to be a small steam engine—the whole affair perhaps ten inches long and five high.

"Now, what is it?" he said.

"I don't know. Looks like a patent model of a steam engine."

He shook his head.

It was a Stirling engine. Designed and patented by a Mr. Stirling, a Scottish minister of religion, in the eighteenth century.

The engine worked, he explained, on heat. Heat was applied to a cylinder, the resultant expansion inside the cylinder moved a valve, thus creating a vacuum inside the cylinder, which vacuum drew a reciprocating valve.

Its efficiency, he explained, was only 6 percent—considerably lower than a steam engine—and for two hundred years engineers had searched in vain for an application.

Then one day, he said, someone observed that the reverse of its inefficiency as an engine was its efficiency as a heat pump—and a variation is now in use extracting the heat given off by supercomputers.

It was a beautiful machine. But I thought it excessive, calling it the most beautiful object he had ever seen.

Reflection suggested, however, its beauty rested not just in the engine-as-such, but in the engine-and-its-history—for it took two hundred years of thought for its simplicity and worth to be recognized, and then the stone which the builders rejected had become the cornerstone, the fast-moving, self-important world came back to Scotland.

Knives

I can't abide stainless steel. It gives me the fantods.

I will accept it in a toaster, but I can't see that it has any place in the blade of a knife.

W. Grigg used to work for Randall's in Orlando, and he offered, first through them and then independently, the finest Daddy Barlow I've ever seen. It was massive—had a lockback that walked and talked as if it were made for NASA, ivory scales, and, unfortunately, a stainless steel blade. It reduced the status of the knife, for me, from that of a superb tool to that of a superb artifact—like a down-filled Hawaiian shirt. What has "progress" brought us to?

What in the world, I ask, is the stuff good for?

Compare today's stainless sheath and pocket knives with the universally available mass-market products of the twenties and thirties, and it makes one want to cry.

Those old, gray-mottled blades would *cut*. (I've got one in my pocket now, a Victorian Joseph Rodgers four-blade congress jack. Dirty stag scales, stained and worn blades, but I can put an edge on it, and it will shave hairs.)

The stainless steel knife just doesn't feel right to me. I put it on a stone and feel like I'm trying to sharpen the front fender of a Chevy. It just doesn't want to cooperate.

But, then, I was ruined from the first. I bought one of those eleven-dollar Russell belt knives out of the Herter's catalogue in the fifties, and that was and is a knife. Great steel, shaped to the hand, no guard, just the blade and full tang, with the wood scales riveted on. I found a replacement three years ago at the Morrisville Gun Show for four bucks, and I treasure it.

The only other real bargain I ever found was at a trading venue called Mud City near Stowe some fifteen years back. There was a Russell Daddy Barlow in bone, in what I'd call excellent shape, for three dollars. I used it for a year, and then sold it through the mail to a well-known trader, and soon thereafter saw it on the cover of a knife magazine. Wish I'd kept it. Oh well.

I was sick some years ago, and laid up in bed with, for some reason, a knife magazine on the bedside table; and to pass the time I wrote away to all the custom makers mentioned therein, and, eventually, did business with a few of them.

Notable among the lot was Bill Bagwell, who became a friend and hunting companion (as I look across at the Glenwood stove I see beneath it a Bagwell-marked goat's-head fire poker he made me one evening at the forge out back of his east Texas home).

Bill ruined me for both stainless steel and the stock-removal method (making knives by grinding down the metal blank).

I've watched Bill forge his knives by hand, packing the blade here, lightening it there, and watched them cut, and they're no joke. One of his more dramatic demonstrations consists in tying four one-inch-diameter rods together and hacking through the four with one swipe of a bowie.

He has also been kind enough to give me sharpening lessons, for which I am grateful.

Like many knife-makers (like many crafts people, for that matter), Bill is a contrarian. He sharpens a blade in a manner exactly opposite to that which I (and you) have been told and have read in every magazine and pamphlet. He drags the blade *away* from the cutting edge, until it turns over a wire edge onto the reverse side, and then *very* gently wipes the wire edge off.

And then he uses the knife to chop through a two-by-six, and then shave hairs.

Quite a demonstration. Which brings us back to the purpose of the instrument in the first place. It's meant to cut.

If the knife won't take an edge, if it won't *hold* an edge, why in the world would one carry it? I believe many of us have had the experience of being in the woods and shaving a stick or two for kindling and finding the knife dull. What a maddening bore, and how it widens one's vocabulary.

And a pocketknife can always be relied on in the woods, if for nothing else than to get itself lost.

I grew up in the era just predating that of the Buckknife, and have never quite been able to reconcile myself to the belt-sheath for a pocketknife. The idea reminds me of the German Forester's Knife—the folding sheath knife so beloved of the European mind.

I say get in or get out. If it's a sheath knife, wear it on a sheath. If it's a folding knife, put it in a pocket.

Yes, it eventually *will* get lost, but in the meantime you don't have to walk around looking like Mr. Peepers, with the cutlery equivalent of the pocket-protector on your belt.

The pocketknife should be in the pocket. The Victorians said one gentleman should never ask "Have you the time?" or "May I borrow your knife" of another; he should have his own knife and watch. And I concur. Carry the pocketknife in the pocket, and when it goes missing, get another one.

Most junk shops, and low-end antique stores, have a display case in which one can find a good, cheap old nonstainless pocketknife.

There are a lot of people making lovely custom folders. I've had a few myself, and first they end up in the wash, and then they end up on the moon with eighteen minutes of Rosemary Woods' tapes.

When I started collecting one could see, at a mid-level New York antique show, Wostenholn and Rodgers bowie knives, emblazoned DEATH TO SLAVERY, DEATH TO ABOLITION, HUNTER'S COMPANION, CALIFORNIA KNIFE, and all the other mottos of the Victorian export trade—beautiful pieces of history for a few hundred dollars. And I still kick myself. I didn't buy them. One could see the Will and Fink San Francisco daggers, or prostitute's knives, Wade and Butcher folding dirks, and so on; which articles have now gone to visit the Quality in the museums, or the Butterfield arms auction.

My collection is a bit more utilitarian. I've got some good R. H. Ruana pieces, a couple of Marbles IDEAL, a Remington U.M.C. on the same pattern (perhaps it was made by Marbles), hunting knives, camp knives, and bowies from Mr. Bagwell, and a box full of old folders, unremarkable save for the I.X.L. pearl-handled advertising knife, which has gone missing, and an ivory-scaled Victorian gentleman's knife, which I just opened before me.

This is the finest pocketknife I've ever seen. It has a three-inch lockback main blade in a modified spear, a penblade, a corkscrew, a buttonhook, an awl, toothpick, scissors, nail file, and tweezers. It all fits together in rather a sleeve-board pattern, and the silver escutcheon plate is inscribed "Sir H. H. Pollock, Bart."

And it is cute as a button, and almost might make one entertain the notion of a belt-sheath for a pocketknife.

It is marked "Thomas Turner and Co. Suffolk Works," and it is pretty damned sweet. The accoutrements fit in tightly and unobtrusively, and are made for use.

It is the opposite of the Swiss Army knives, those all-purpose instruments which seem to be handy for anything save cutting.

I am not a fan of the multipurpose tool. The genre seems to me, in the main, 'morphadite rigs which might do a bit of a few jobs, and then contribute to the entertainment of the situation by breaking.

An exception: I remember Randall's used to advertise (their current literature advises me they still do) that they would fit a small compass into a knife's butt-cap—a style pioneered by Bradford Angier, I believe. I thought this rather a *cheechako* affectation until the first time I got myself no-joke lost in the woods. Currently I think there is no pocket or tool which would not be improved by the addendum of a compass.

But, finally, both the beauty and the utility of any instrument depend on the single-mindedness and talent of the designer in fitting the tool to the task.

Which brings us back to philosophy. I can use my pocketknives as handy lifters to open the woodstove; when I carried a Buckknife I found the brass bolster made a good hammer; the Swiss Army knife is, as we know, great for removing a splinter, but, at the end of the day, the purpose of a knife is to cut. To that end it should be made of steel designed to cut, it should be (preferably) forged and/or ground into a shape suitable for the sort of cutting intended, and the blade should be set in a handle ergonomically correct for the tasks at hand.

Mr. Bagwell advises (and carries) a large (nine-to-twelve-inch) bowie in the woods. It is not a macho overcompensation. It's not there to skin deer or to dissuade or subdue malefactors, it's a substitute for the hand ax, and it does the job right smartly. For the camp chores, including skinning, he carries a five- or six-inch camp knife, and so do I.

I'm talking about a small, single-edged (probably drop-point) narrow-tang utility knife, with, probably, a half-guard. It can whittle a fuzz-tree, or a tent peg, lift a pot off the fire, or dress a deer, and how many other tools can make that statement?

We all have various clothing and gear that looks pretty, but we take items into the woods because we're confident in them, and if they don't function as required, we don't take them again. So I take a Bagwell camp knife, and slip a traitorous pocketknife into a pocket or two, and, probably, put an old Marbles Safety Ax into the pack. (The bowie knife, I do allow, does the job better, but we all saw too many articles in too many magazines over the years by a chap who dressed out an elk with a pocket comb; and I wouldn't want to meet that fellow on the trail and feel called upon to explain myself. Is this a character defect? Definitely.)

On the city street I slip an old Robeson or Rodgers, or a Case Serpentine jack, into a pocket. (All my custom-folders—Cenofante, Bagwell-Pardue, Teruzola, etc.—as I said, have ended on the Moon.)

A word about browsing.

As a kid I enjoyed the gun-and-knife rooms at Marshall Field's Men's Store and, down Wabash Avenue, at Abercrombie and Fitch/V.L. + A, at which last store I bought my first Randall knife out of the case—a bird-and-trout knife, long since gone. I am pleased to note and to report that the same spirit of informed and friendly assistance I found then seems to live on at Stoddards Cutlery in Boston, at Paragon Sports knife department in New York, through Bruce Voyles, and through A. G. Russell's various mail-order enterprises, and at the New York Custom Knife Show—some modern and urban versions of the Courthouse Lawn.

I've enjoyed collecting knives. I wish I'd kept an example of the Grigg Daddy Barlow I decried at the beginning. It was a work of art.

I wish I'd bought that California bowie at the New York Knife Show, and the decrepit, rusted Randall fighter a fellow had for sale in Hyder, Alaska. It was coming apart, the leather washers were eaten through, but it had been around, and the sheath was marked H. HEISER. We differed by five dollars, and the knife is probably still up there.

What would I have done with it? I would have sent it to Randall's, asked them to refurbish it, carried it once or twice. Someone might say it would then be forgotten in my closet rather than living in my memory.

I like a knife that will stain. I like it to show wear. I like it to have a story—that, after all, is the joy of collecting, to understand the story. The joy of use is to add to it.

Caps

I should like to take issue with the notion that "one size fits all." I think it an enormity and an imposition. I refer to caps. It is a style largely observed in urban youth, which seems to've spread around the country: that of the cap turned backward.

I do not know what it portends in its more modern appearance, but, of old, it was the appurtenance and right of the motion picture cameraman and director.

Motion pictures, in the early years, were shot on slow (not very light-sensitive) stock. They were, therefore, shot outdoors.

One needed a cap to keep the glare out. On approaching the camera one turned the cap backwards; and if one, on quitting the camera, forgot, for a time, to reverse the cap into its more ordinary position, if one, in effect, awarded oneself a prolonged distinction of office, well, wasn't that a harmless thing?

I have been fortunate, at times, to have directed motion pictures, and it never failed to delight me, this reversing-of-the-cap. How technical, how work-a-day and yet romantic. Where else is it done save in the address to the periscope?

But now we have these one-size-fits-all caps. They sport, at the back, a plastic contrivance which no wise could be construed romantic either in construction or material. It might, in fact, derive from, and it might in fact double as, a closure on a trash bag. It is cheap, and it is ugly. Reversing it upon the head creates a mockery of a Palladian overdoor upon the forehead, and I do not like it at all. I prefer old caps.

Photographs

We did not, in the City, in my youth, wear blue jeans. They were called "dungarees" and were acceptable attire only on someone actually working in a garden.

All adults smoked. My parents smoked while at the table, between bites of food.

The 1950s museum would contain a child's eye, which had been put out by a BB gun; an electric toaster which killed a kid who'd stuck a fork into it; a child whose friends had all jumped off the Empire State Building; several Chinese saved from starvation when an American Kid finished his vegetables.

Captain Video and his video rangers aired every evening, if memory served, at five, or five-fifteen, and followed or were followed by *Kukla, Fran, and Ollie,* that magnificent, impro-vised-live-five-times-a-week comedy drama featuring Kukla the Clown and his friend, Ollie the Dragon, hand puppets under the direction of the great Burr Tillstrom.

The automobiles at the time seemed to me enormous; and, forty years later, they still seem so. I remember my father's taste for Buick, and I remember thinking even then, Surely he can't think the holes-in-the-side have any practical value.

I remember one of his clients drove a Hudson, and that this was worthy of some regular note around our house, though I cannot remember why.

I remember we boys knew the model name of every new car, soon as it came out.

We had a world of boys. Three seasons we would take the el to Comiskey Park to see Nellie Fox, or Luis Aparicio; or up to Wrigley Field to see Ernie Banks.

Winters my dad would take me, now and then, to see the Bears, who still played, then, at Soldier Field. That was some cold.

We learned, liberals like myself, learning in the sixties and since, to derogate that time as one of moral lethargy and reaction. Perhaps it was so.

Looking at photographs, I see and I remember a naiveté or perhaps a peace unimaginable today.

Where is the protected peace and quiet of those middle-class streets?

Where is the Ruritanian-quaint happiness of the after-work Loop, the stores open late, the restaurants thronged with families out to stroll, on their way to a movie, window-shopping?

My parents' generation worked hard. They were, in my neighborhood, the children of immigrants; they had survived the Depression and the Second World War. They worked to gain admittance to school—most struggling additionally against anti-Jewish quotas—and they worked to succeed in their business or profession.

We, in the sixties, lived out what might have been their generation's vision—not a dream, or even a fantasy, but a hallucination of entitlement and license.

We took for granted those things they had toiled to grant us.

And I and other parents of my age strive, as do parents in any age, to give our children what we did not have.

Our parents strove to give us plenty, perhaps we strive to give our children peace.

I remember listening to adults, and, indeed, to children born just slightly before me, listening to them reminisce about the Age of Radio.

I listened to them longingly.

I look back to the naiveté of the early television years not with longing—it was always an addiction at best, and any content was accidental and, I think, finally worthless, as part of a bargain with addiction—not with longing but with a certain disbelief. Couldn't we (they) tell, I wonder, where this all would lead?

The air and the water and the cities grow worse every day, and the electronic answer, the anodyne, is not their amelioration but a narcotizing of the mind and will. The devilish ability of the media to demand attention grows in proportion to our need for oblivion. The screen screams at us to be immobile and thoughtless, and to understand this immobility as education, entertainment, work.

It screams like the two hundred thousand demons assailing the Buddha as he sat beneath the Po tree. And, like those demons, everything it screams is a lie. Punching the buttons is not work.

Watching the predigested "presentations" is not education but indoctrination to slavery—it *is* slavery—and x-hundred choices of "entertainment" do not entertain but *demand* our attention. They leave us not refreshed but tired, not piqued but uninterested, and we teach ourselves to call this interaction happy.

Society has always been ruled by the hegemony controlling the high ground, the crossroads, the harbor, the means of human intercourse.

Traditionally we have been controlled by the group first with the new means of warfare—the horse, the crossbow, firearms, cast cannon, et cetera.

Of late the high ground and the crossroads both are becoming the air, and the control of the images sent through it.

The group in control can compel purchase, political action, and most activities else or in between.

Where is the peace in the amalgamation of power? Where is the possibility of peace in the growth of the antiliteracy it embodies and spreads?

We live in an age of confusion, and are told and tell each other it is ordered by some magic quality called "information."

But where is the romance in it? Where is the discovery?

Facing the works of God we *wonder*—they are beyond our imagining—quite exactly the reverse of information.

Facing even the most magnificent of human works we are prone to approve, applaud, in some way strive to make ourselves equal with them—to equate an act of appreciation with an act of creation—a choice which the natural universe does not afford us. That is the reason we find such natural interactions cleansing.

To deal with the world, as difficult as it may be, is to lay down the burden of self. To attempt to reorder the world, to recast all of its secrets into a personally accessible form, is psychosis—the act of one forced by horror to retreat.

I look at the photographs of my childhood and see adult faces marked by toil.

I see that generation today, retirees in their campers and trailers, on summer highways, enjoying the leisure they earned with their fifty years of toil.

My generation's rest will be worried, harried, and begrudged. Well, then, this was my generation's time.

There was nothing romantic in it, and the howlings of the television to the contrary only serve to prove the point.

Our generation will be found to have grinned at the camera in a disingenuous attempt to convince someone of our ease, mugging for all the world like a bad television actor.

The New House

My parents renovated an apartment and lived in it for thirty years. I thought of it as "the new apartment" until my father's death, when I saw it was old, outdated, and worn.

It must have been, for it had been lived in for thirty years.

The fellow wrote, "It takes a heap o' living to make a house a home"; and the transition comes, like most of the important ones in life, when our attention is elsewhere—either on the unremarkable day-to-day business of living or on demanding ritual, which is a mechanism designed to take its place.

The traumatic transition from single to married bliss is meant to occur with the participants occupied in sexual anticipation or frenzy, the painful and seemingly endless period of acclimatization to divorce to be moderated by an otherwise inexplicable interest in persons unsuitable for companionship. The shock of life with a new baby is lessened during and by the wonderful narcotic of sleeplessness.

In the tragic instances, of course, the stress of disruption is magnified by loss; but the simple disruption of habit, even in the happiest of situations, can cause stress, for example, the much-noted return from the vacation.

Habit, William James informed us, allows us to raise our thoughts and spirits from the mechanical—it allows our thoughts to wander; and, in fact, the obsessive-compulsive individual artificially supplies a demanding mechanical necessity in order to protect him- or herself against free-ranging thoughts.

When the habitual is, at a stroke, destroyed, our mind is forced to occupy itself with the mundane, the minuscule. The simplest unconscious act—crossing the street—becomes conscious and, so, difficult, as those who shuttle between the U.K. and the right-driving world can testify: "What country am I in, and from which direction must traffic, therefore, be coming?"

When one moves, the ten thousand daily choices which have become habitual through that "heap o' living" are still pressing to be made, but must be made consciously, their very insignificance a trial.

The large associations—where Sarah told me she was pregnant, the couch where Buffy always went when she skinned her knee, the drawer where Boots had kittens—are lumped in with the small: where the hell are the spoons? The move consigns the large and the small into one pathetic stew. The mind is, then, not free to order the environment; the previously unconscious becomes conscious, plodding, and regrettable, and life at home is no longer easy. The conscious mind suggests that the situation is inevitable, that one has just moved, but the unconscious ripostes: well and good, but couldn't one have moved into the place where one previously *lived?*

In the move our attention is continually forced to an order we had accepted as natural but which is revealed, in its disruption, to have been only artificial, essentially or originally arbitrary, and sustained only by habit.

We see that we shall have to begin all over again and that our treasured peace (or *pace*, the neurotic household, trauma) was a product of time and work.

I once asked a psychiatrist how it came about that intelligent, kind, perceptive people, when convened into a family, could devote themselves to ongoing, nay, eternal, silly quarrels.

He smiled and said the quarrels were the landing lights at the airport: they let the travelers know they'd arrived home.

Well, we move, and much has to begin again.

Treasured associations *will* emerge, and our efforts to speed them will not be of much avail.

Transplanted pettinesses may be revealed as extraneous and discarded or renewed with a sigh.

(My Rabbi tells a story of a newcomer to the congregation. He watched as worshippers, walking to the front of the *shul*, stooped almost into a duck-walk at one point in the procession. The new fellow did likewise. After a year he asked a congregant what the religious significance was of that walk. The old-timer thought a minute, then said, "Oh. There used to be a heating duct there.")

Stanislavsky wrote that the difficult must become easy and the easy habitual before the habitual can become beautiful. And so it is, of course, with the new house, and no amount of denigrating our affection for the spot where Maisy dinged the doorjamb with her trike will lessen its significance.

As I age I begin to see the sense of the archetype of the crotchety old man or old woman—they become or can become cantankerous as they are chided at every turn by knowledge that the thing is finite.

Much of the stress of moving is caused by the enforced notice of the passage of time.

I did a film with an extraordinary actor, a movie star of the forties.

He was eighty-one. He didn't look it; he worked and laughed and futzed around as an equal participant in that wonderful jumble of work-play which is a film set.

Then he began to get a bit cantankerous, and I wondered why. I realized we were two days from the end of shooting, at which point he was going to be translated from an ageless member and full participant in the world's best club to a life where everything and anything had the potential of suggesting to him that he was an old man.

As I age I see my potential for pique at the inconsequential increase. Much of it, of course, is plain bad manners or lack of philosophy. On my behalf I might, however, suggest the mitigating irritations of the intimations of mortality in the banal.

For example, if the shovel breaks and I trudge off to replace it, well, I might be testy. And perhaps I might be so because the shovel has associations.

Might I *not* be equally testy, however, because and as it be-

came clear to me that this shovel, this new shovel, this trai-
tor, was odds-on a favorite to be the last that I might buy?

And if true of garden tools, what of the New House?

On the one hand one might devoutly wish it to be that
house in which one might live out one's life—but if it *were*,
must that not mean that life is not only finite but evapo-
rating?

And if or as we are getting toward, or—it may be—well
into, the last portion of the race, must it not mean that one
can never be a fireman?

(My wonderful Grandmother Clara, rest in peace, would ask
me what I wanted to be, and I would always tell her that I
wished to be a fireman. In my youth my affections did not
that way tend, and I chose another career and have become
stuck with it. I have a friend who, at the age of fifty, dedicated himself to the volunteer fire department of his adopted
New England town, and it seems to've changed his life. I tell
myself that my job entails travel sufficient to debar me from
a similar renewal and fantasize about creating for myself a
volunteer position tailored to both my special needs and, if I
may, my skills—that of consulting fireman. To wit: "Hello?
Yes. Can you describe it to me? All right. When you get *close* to
it, is it 'warm'? Aha. Well, I'm going to tell you what you've *got*
there, but first I'm going to give you a number I'd like you to
call. Got a pencil . . . ?") But I digress.

The New House would, one hopes, be that bulwark, that
"friend to whom the shadow of far years extends."

But while and were they to so extend, would they not
make that extension to a domicile empty of one's so spiri-
tually generous self?

And, then, what is the point of the whole exercise in this new, foreign hulk which cost a fortune, where one cannot locate the tea, and which hulk may be nothing more than a dormitory for those ignorant of and unsympathetic to one's sacrifice, one's anomie, et cetera? Oh, boo hoo.

Well, in my family we are blessed to say that as long as we have each other we could live in a packing crate—and, equally, one should never ask sympathy for a man with a solarium, and so I beg your pardon.

The days will come and the days will go. I will or will not be there to see them, and I hope my children will have the diversion of looking at the house and wondering how we could have persisted in considering it new when it had become, any outsider could see it, aged and used long, long ago.

Producers

The truest joke about Hollywood is that in which a writer, a producer, and a director are marooned in the desert. The writer discovers a long-buried can of tomato juice, the director manages to open it, the producer takes it and says, "I am going to divide the contents into three equal parts— but first I'm going to piss in it."

The funniest joke about producers I found in a biography of David O. Selznick. The biographer referred to a shot of Jennifer Jones, saying it was the most striking in all of Selznick's work.

The joke is that the film was *not* his work. To refer to a producer's oeuvre is, at least to me, as ignorant as to refer to the oeuvre of a stockbroker.

Mencken wrote that government was brokerage in pillage, and so, it seems to me, is the work of the so-called producer.

The position, especially in films, is one of the huckster, an intermediary, extorting or cajoling funds from the rich and work from the creative.

Now, this person would not be, and is not, a bad associ- ate from time to time. One of my best friends, unfortu- nately, is a producer, for whose sake one might be tempted to spare the city of Sodom. But to call the function of the producer part of the artistic "work" is ludicrous.

Whatever property producers control, and however much money they may have to entice, the work is done by the artist, and however much the artist might find him- or her- self at a loss in the marketplace, it is as nothing compared with the impotence of the producer facing a blank page.

And most of them are thieves. Like the lazy rich occupy- ing themselves with real or, more frequently, imagined pec- ulations on the part of the help, the producers I have met have, in the main, been dedicated to a form of reactive or pre-emptive revenge, defrauding the artist both of money and time.

I was once involved in directing a television show.

The contracts were not executed, and I was halfway through the work, having proceeded on a handshake deal, when the producer announced he was going to cut my pay in half.

"But we have an agreement," I said.

"Well, costs have risen," he said.

"But we have an agreement," I said.

"Wait, wait, wait," he said, "do you expect me to *pay* for the privilege of working with you . . . ?"

I had to laugh. The fellow was a cheat, but he'd framed his riposte as, I then fully understood, the essential and pervasive outrage of the producer: "Don't these lazy people know what I go *through . . . ?*"

Well, no, I don't. And I don't care.

It may be true in any business, but I know it is true in show business: the entrepreneur feels, nay *knows,* himself entitled to extract, extort, and cheat anything from the, to his mind, worthless wretch he has rescued from poverty.

Producers consider themselves, I know, like those South African overseers passing out bologna to the natives who spend their lives in the river searching for an emerald.

"Well," they must think, "if they wanted to get out of the river, they should have gone to law school like me."

Now, through my life I have both pined and searched for that paragon of whom I read, that Diaghilev, Nemirovich-Danchenko, or Lincoln Kirstein who would find the funds, support my aims, and relieve me of all burdens I found the least objectionable.

And I have been fortunate to have, in fact, experienced such relationships—more usually in the theatre but even, now and then, in films.

I was and am, I hope, grateful for these periods of support and honesty; I know they were more precious to me for their rarity.

"What," one may ask, "do you, the artist, expect? Do you expect *gratitude?*"

The answer, of course, is "yes." I would not only accept but would be thrilled with honesty, whether as an expression of gratitude or of self-respect; but, yes, I do expect (and have occasionally received) gratitude.

Does this make me an egoist? I don't know. I may or may

not be, and the apposition of the term to me is not going to be affected by this minute confession. I am grateful for the funds supplied to enable me to work—I'm sure most artists are. I try to express that gratitude through sticking to the letter and the spirit of the bargain. (I don't think I'm unique in this, I think it is how most, perhaps all, artists behave.) Am I deluded to expect a reciprocal gratitude, expressed in a similar devotion to both the letter and the spirit of the producer's end of the bargain?

And, then, we must remember, although it is the age-old saw of the entrepreneur, "I paid your rent, I gave you your break," the opposite is at least equally true: that without the artist, the entrepreneur, the producer, the broker-in-hyperbole, would starve; that while it is by no means impossible (or unheard of) that the artist lay down the pencil or the brush and go out into the world to produce, distribute, exhibit his or her own works, it is beyond fantasy that so-called producers, absent a complaisant artist, could support themselves through an act of creation.

And yet, the artist tends, in my experience, to court, to defer to, to retreat before, and to brook the depredations, the lies, and the thefts of the producer.

"Let me take your cow to market for you, son," the highwayman says.

And, certainly, the way to market is and has always been dangerous.

One could meet, on that road, the confidence man, the thief, and on arrival at the marketplace one could meet, in addition, the entrepreneur, willing to blur and to cross the line between business, sharp practice, and outright theft.

In the modern producer one can meet them all.

And, yes, there are exceptions I have found, and you may find them, too.

But, most often, you will find false promises, evasions, lies, short weight, slow pay, cooked books, and, perhaps, even vexatious litigation, perjury, and peculation of funds. I unfortunately speak from experience.

"But you've done right well in show business," one might say. In which I might reservedly concur, always thanking (and that, I hope, at something approximating their full contribution) those forces responsible.

But none of them is a producer.

L.A. Homes

We call each other up at night and trade our horror stories.

"The movie star called and said he had to meet me. We made a date for the Ivy at one. He showed up at one-forty-five. 'Had trouble finding a parking space,' he said.

His hair was wet.

We talked for twenty minutes about everything other than the project. The check came.

There was a long, long pause. 'I'll get it,' I said. We got up to go. 'They validate parking here?' he asked.

'I'm sure I don't know,' I said. Asked the waiter. The waiter said, 'no.' 'Left my wallet at home,' he said. Another long pause. 'Do you need to borrow some money?' I asked. 'Yes,' he said. I lent him twenty bucks."

"Went to an audition," another friend said. "Did a great job. I thought. Fellow's eyes glaze over. 'Is there something else you'd like me to do,' I asked, 'or that you'd like me to do differently?'

'No,' he said. 'Not at all.'

'Yes . . . ?'

'It's. . . . you're too *real*,' he said.

'Too real . . .' I said.

'Yes,' he said.

'What does that mean?' I said.

'We need,' he said. 'We need a real *babe* for this part.'

'What does that mean?' I said.

'You're not pretty enough,'"

A producer calls up. "What a script," he says. "You have written a *script*—we had the first reading today, I wish you'd have been there. If we'd *video'd* it, we could have released *that*. The *hell* with the film . . . the electricity in the room . . . your *words*." He paused.

"Yes?" I said.

"There's only one problem," he said.

"What?" I said.

"Jack doesn't like the plot."

It's, of course, what hell must be like, if hell has valet parking.

But here is the rub: what about their *homes?*

In Chicago "come by for dinner" meant come by at *six*, we'll all eat at the Formica kitchen table, the kids'll be running around, and so on.

I went to New York and "come for dinner" meant dress up, the invitation is for nine, we'll start drinking, the drinks will be passed around by caterers, we'll eat at eleven, a sit-down affair with place cards.

The dining room will be tastefully overdecorated, you'll be so drunk you won't care.

In L.A. they say "come by" and the dinner is served, at the top of the food chain, by wonderfully informal and correct staff, the food isn't bad, but the insupportable, true enormity is that the house is lovely.

What are these savages doing in these lovely homes? I wonder.

For the homes are actually lovely.

In Chicago we referred to the *charge de décor* as the "dreck-erator"; and I was pleased, both for myself and for the prescience of my race, to discover that Frank Lloyd Wright referred to the metier as "desecrator," and that, with few exceptions, has been my experience—but those L.A. houses, well, they were swell. The abodes of the studio heads and the hotshot producers—they showed, and one felt, what Edith Wharton referred to as "the demoralizing simplicity of great wealth." There one was, in the Greene and Greene Bungalow, the Craftsman Gothic, the Japanese Bungalow, the most charming, trig, airy, and light houses.

How dare they?

How dare these Visigoths who used terms like "moral dilemma" and "flavor-of-the-month," who demanded various young women strip to the buff to audition for a voice-over, who went white-water rafting down the Colorado with their ilk to "bond," who said "ecksetera," how *dare* they have a home in which one found American Art Pottery?

I had a very famous director call me and ask if I'd be interested in writing a new screenplay of *Moby Dick.* "Sure thing," I said.

"One change," he said. "We want you to write it from the point of view of the whale."

And yet this race of vandals does not find itself incapable of hanging on the wall the Charlie Russel watercolor or the odd run of Grueby tiles or of employing decorators who've revived the taste for Stickley and Elbert Hubbard, who did not found Dianetics, or whatever it's called.

These folks, who greenlit or greenlighted blah blah blah part Eye Vee, should display the proverbial moose-on-satin with the eyes which follow one about. These people should, by rights, have the bullfight poster with one's name upon it hanging in the john INSTEAD OF WHICH we find the pure, unscented handmade soap from some off-brand country lying, pristine, in the small, green Hampshire soap dish. Well, Meredith Willson said it best: "Make your blood boil? Well, I should say."

Now, friends, let me tell you what I mean. How dare these anti-literate traffic-cops at the roadside crash which is our culture, how dare they *dare* to have anything around them which is lovely?

I have seen a room of perfect proportions, with the pickled floor and the requisite French country table on which were three Teco jugs. This in the house of a producer who in any sane land would be doing community service in an urn.

I have seen an Ellsworth Kelly in the kitchen of a man who said, on my script on the Spanish Civil War, "not enough Spaniards."

I know these folk, the beloved thugs of the ongoing aesthetic morality tale which, to us in the arts, is our hero-journey. I know these Mamelukes of Mammon, I say, have only gone out and bought a decorator. I know that. But nonetheless.

And I know Hitler hired Leni Riefenstahl, and she made a couple of compelling flicks, but hey.

But how dare they, once again? And what can it do to my sensitive soul to see examples of *both* the Saturday Evening Girls and Newcomb College Potters on the sideboard of a man who watched the dailies of my films *in his limo*, while talking on the phone, to see a wheat-tangerine Heriz on the floor of the man who said of my (rejected) script for *Lolita*: "You made him look like a pedophile"?

A black year on Columbus.

The cars are tasteful, the food is tasteful, the homes are tasteful, the clothing is tasteful, and you wouldn't spend a weekend with these folks to save Eleanor Roosevelt.

What would one *talk* about? And what could be worse than discovering that the purveyor of Entertainment so wholesome as to be proof against criticism of anything up to but not including its content knew and could compare-and-contrast the slip glaze on a Rookwood vase with the foliated decoration (by Ruth Erikson) on one by Grueby Faience.

It was like Martin Bormann chanting Talmud.

It's not right.

There is no seam in it. It is beyond bearing.

It will be like the day when we're told Martha Stewart's found the AIDS cure.

The dog of the day: The Golden, or the English-bred, Lab; the German Drathaar or the Italian Spinetti; the Range Rover or sixties Ford pickup; the Yohji jacket, the quarter-sawn oak, the yellow Formica breakfast table and chairs in the kitchen which (*eppur si muove*) could have been at my aunt's house. And as I write it occurs to me, as it occurs to you, the rejoinder of the bloke discovered at the whorehouse: "You couldn't have seen me if you weren't there yourself." And, of course, I was, and looked on the pottery and the car and the jacket and the dog with longing born of a desire for the End of Strife.

Yes, you might say, here is a fellow we have caught in the whorehouse.

He has too much time on his hands, and is envying the neighbor's bric-a-brac and trying to denominate it outraged aestheticism.

What a sell!

So I reveal myself. I do it for a living, and perhaps it is the most elastic application of chaos theory to blame Creative Artists Agency for the unpalatable increase in the price of McCoy pottery, but, in the words of Marlene Dietrich, "Caaaan't help it."

Finally, Hollywood is, of course, a company town.

And any company town is designed like an inverted boat—we find the ballast at the top.

And so we may say the Beacon blanket, the attendant Grenfell rug, the fugitive-green quilt, the Traulsen fridge, the early Mennonite pine tables of Santa Monica are the anomalous equivalent of the fabled white plastic belt and glass drinks-cart of Grosse Point, Michigan. That's just the way it is, that's just the way These People Live, and when they die, they'll probably, things being what they are, go straight to heaven, and it will be the lounge of the Admiral's Club, and they'll like that just fine, too.

Karmann Ghia

My first car was a 1967 Karmann Ghia.

I bought it in 1972 for nine hundred dollars.

It went like a bat out of hell on the back roads of Vermont, and it just sat down into the turns, and loved to corner.

I will permit myself the license of a onetime American Boy and suggest the car operated like a good bird dog out in the field: it got the idea and it wanted to help.

I loved that car.

I can almost remember the moment I stopped thinking it ugly and recognized it as revelation in design.

I think it ranks with and perhaps surpasses the bathtub Porsche for perfection of line.

(It seems they were both designed by the same fellow. And aficionados, over the years, told me they were largely the same machine—different body, smaller engine, of course, in the Ghia . . .)

It would go all day, and did.

I was living in Montpelier, Vermont, and courting a young lady in New Haven, and I seem to remember making the trip in two and three-quarter hours.

I know it can't quite be true, even given the legal limit of seventy-five miles per hour, and the insistent pheromones of that time, but that's what I remember.

And the car would plow snow.

I'd go out in the Vermont winter morning to find a turtle-shaped mound of snow out on the street.

I'd broom it off, turn the engine over (it caught, as the car of one's youth must of course do, first time, every time), and plow through snow over the front bumper, the twenty miles to work, when nothing else on the road moved.

The perfect car.

I drove it to Chicago and back several times.

It did not, I will admit, like the Alleghenies very well, but which of us is perfect?

It was beige, and the top was black.

The Ghia literature of that time described the beige as desert sand. Other colors of that make and era include a dark, almost Chinese, red and British Racing green.

You may recall the avatar of the Ghia line at that period—the Ghia convertible—British Racing green body, black top.

I would, at times, wonder whether that car was superior to my two-tone hardtop, only for the joy of arriving at the correct solution—that *no* car was superior to mine. Not the convertible, not the 1800 Volvo, not the 3000 Austin-Healy—not even that era's original Toyota Land Cruiser, which looked like the Jeep's Good Big Brother.

I was teaching drama at a small Vermont college. Getting paid several hundred dollars for a month of eighteen-hour days, and having the time of my life.

My needs were few, and all of them were being met when a new bar opened in Montpelier and we found the bartender could mix a drink.

So my pals and I would close the joint every night.

(I particularly remember it as the heyday of the Tequila Sunrise—the Singapore Sling or Sloe Gin Fizz of the seventies.)

So the bartender drove the cost of living up, and I applied to the college for a slight raise.

The faculty board called me in and berated me. "How can you say," they said, "you need money to live when you have just purchased an expensive luxury sports car?"

They say the definition of ambivalence is watching your mother-in-law drive over a cliff in your new Cadillac. But I adore my mother-in-law, so I vote for my feelings toward that college board as a conclusive definition.

Consumed with rage comma (as *Time* magazine taught us to write) and filled with pride, I did not know whether to mow the grass or write home to Mother; but I spurted out to that faculty board, "But the car didn't cost but nine hundred bucks . . ."

In retrospect, it was not, of course, the car to which they objected but my youth, and my enjoyment of it. Is it crass to so-report?

Perhaps, but it's true.

And a large proportion of enjoyment, nay, delight, came from that car.

The windshield wipers didn't work. No amount of restoration or remedy was capable of overcoming what seemed to be the car's only real design flaw.

The wiper arms had a small square mortise—if that is the word—that fit down over a square drive peg.

The peg twisted to cause the arms to move and, in twisting, galled and chafed through the soft metal so that, quickly, when one turned the wipers on, one heard the whine and saw them twist, attempt to rise, and fall back on their bed like a faithful dog who (*you* finish it).

But who required wipers who possessed a driver's license?

For, in Vermont, anytime it rained it was likely to snow, and when it snowed, I could drive those twenty miles, as I did, that many a day and night, my left hand and arm out of the window, scraping a view through the accumulating ice and rime with my Vermont driver's license.

I sold the car when I left the state. I got four hundred bucks for it, and the check bounced.

Eight years later I was jogging down Sunset Boulevard, most probably from the Chateau Marmont to Schwab's (yes, you historians will note, a short run, indeed; I was not very fit in those days). Jogging, I say, when I saw, there, the selfsame car. The '67 Ghia, sand and black, at the curb, and on its windshield a FOR SALE sign.

I called the number and bought the thing for fifteen hundred dollars. I had it trucked back East; and, once again, bat-out-of-hell, sit-down-into-the-turns, the entire lovely repertoire.

But the car began, over the years, to come apart. Not from use but from neglect.

I'd only drive it one or two months a year, and it began to

object in ways which could not be overlooked—the paint, the windshield gaskets, the electric system, et cetera.

I should have had it packed and shrink-wrapped, or whatever one does, and hauled to a car preservation environment—which, as far as I can figure out, is both a job description and the only excuse for the continued existence of Los Angeles. A cheap but accurate shot.

But I could not because, it occurs to me, if the car of my youth had become an antique, what did that say about *me?*

So I sold it. To a delighted buyer. And may it continue to scream around, never needing gas, on the trails of adventure.

Farewell, then, car of my youth, with your fold-down backseat and consequently large luggage compartment; with your *so* many miles a gallon even in the age of American petroleum hegemony; with your stylish European lines; with the alacrity with which you took me courting. Farewell.

As Mr. Kipling said, "We've only one virginity to lose, and where we've lost it, there our Heart will be."

Smash Cut

A friend in Hollywood said he was contemplating the purchase of an obscenely expensive automobile.

"Why?" I said.

"It'll go one hundred and forty miles per hour," he said.

"But, Art," I said. "You never go over forty."

"Yes," he said, "but it's very fast *at* forty."

His comment, like much of the utterance in and around our beloved Versailles, falls into the category of "things which almost mean something."

Shakespeare, writing on spec, said it best: "Brief as the lightening in the collied night, which, ere a man hath power to say 'behold,' the jaws of darkness do devour it up." As we endeavor to parse the phrase, it disappears. These utterances of almost-meaning do serve to communicate information. The information, however, is limited to this: we're all playing Silly Buggers.

Consider the phrase "smash cut." I, and you, have found the same and similar in a screenplay presenting itself as a direction to the editor.

But how would an editor deal with such a direction?

What would "smash cut" mean?

The writer might respond, "Oh, come off it . . . *you* know," and we might nod in complicity or friendship. But what *does* it mean?

Two shots can be joined, if memory serves, by a dissolve, by a fade, or by a cut.

A *cut* involves a scissors and glue, or their postmodern equivalents—the footage of one shot stops, the footage of another shot begins—that's the only way I know or can conceive to do it.

One may cut the film at any point, thus achieving differences in visual content and rhythm (film students take note), but at the end-of-the-day, it's a *cut*, and that's all it is. It can't be soft, violent, slow, or smash. It's a cut.

Some read and still maintain, "What is he *on* about? *I* know what the phrase means." And I respond, no, you do not. You *think* you know what it means; but honest reflection will reveal that it means nothing.

Similarly, the phrase "high-concept"—which finally means "interesting," or, perhaps, "interesting-and-novel." Its employment advertises a claim to expertise on the part of the speaker, which claim is happily absent in the similar "Golly, I'd like to see *that*" of the vulgate.

But there ain't no expertise in "high-concept," there is only arrogance passing itself off, as it will, as inside information.

We see such again in the designation "character-driven."

It is presented as the opposite of "plot-driven," and, after some cogitation, I confess I don't know what it means.

I *think* it means that the project in question has a weak plot.

Consider: for all of the gobbledegook executives spout about "backstory," all that we, the audience, want to know is "what happens next." That's the only thing that's going on.

When the person who went to pee comes back to the couch and the television, they ask, "What's happening?" They mean, and we understand them to mean, only this: tell me facts sufficient to allow me to wonder "what's going to happen next."

There is *plot* (which is the structure of incidents in which the hero/heroine is involved in attempting to accomplish their goal) and there is absence of—weakness of—plot.

Character is nothing other than *action*, and *character-driven* means "the plot stinks, and you better hope the star is popular enough to open the movie in spite of it."

Medieval physicians disputed at length over the curative powers of various gems—whether ground topaz was better for scrofula than amethyst, et cetera.

Studio executives, similarly, frightened by responsibility for events and processes beyond their understanding, create an infra-universe with its own language and logic.

What are Production Values?

I think this phrase means "waste."

The genius of *Jaws* is the ability to terrify us with a shot of empty ocean. The best shot in *Close Encounters* (or any other S.F. film) is the vision of the lights of the car at the railroad crossing rising.

Equally thrilling is the sequence in *The Thing* where the scientists spread out to determine the outlines of the craft beneath the ice and they (and we) discover it to be a saucer.

"Production values," i.e., *waste,* does not thrill us but leaves us feeling empty; like an encounter with a whore, like voting, but I repeat myself. "Production values" means, if a tête-à-tête with a fascinating woman is interesting, lunch with a squad of 'em should be divine—good moviemaking requires not conspicuous expenditure but disciplined imagination.

"Backstory" seems to mean "narration," and the public, coming back from its refreshing trip to the loo, couldn't care less.

As audience, we are as little interested in narration as would be the viewers of a prizefight. Imagine the fighter turning to us to say, "Yes, I am about to get into the ring, but first, I'd like to tell you a few things about myself . . ."

WE JUST DON'T CARE. We, the audience, are paying the fighter, the moviemaker, to GET ON WITH IT. "Backstory" gives the hard-pressed executive something to say beyond "aren't you losing weight?"

The third act could *always* use work. It takes some understanding of dramatic structure to discuss the nature of that work intelligently.

But anything capable of being trained to "want a cracker," can say "I want to know more *about* him."

And what of our beloved "moral dilemma"?

This phrase would seem to have some meaning. If the heroine or hero were involved in a moral dilemma, their solution might aid you or me in our own—pointing the way toward a cleaner, happier, and kinder life.

But I have heard of this "moral dilemma" in offices only. I have never seen it on the screen. Have you?

And what do we do when the executive speaks to us about this dilemma?

We nod humbly (who would want to conspire up front to create a work of immorality?), and then go home and rant to our significant other about the idiot we just had to spend the last hour with.

There is the Problem of the Protagonist. His or her attempts to solve this problem are the PLOT. What *is* this moral dilemma?

It is Jane Austen's widower. "Where is this widower," she writes, "I have heard much about them, but I have never seen one."

The great works of drama of the stage and of melodrama of the flickers are reducible to a concrete problem on the part of the protagonist. "Moral dilemma" is in the same category of utterance as "Mother, may I?" It's used as an obeisance to the bureaucracy.

I love the language of Hollywood. It is as colorful and inventive as that of any other regal or criminal pursuit.

Death, defecation, sex, money—all the big ones demand and receive their own burgeoning vocabulary; they reduce us to a primitive-infantile state.

The military changes killed-in-action to "K.I.A." to kilo-india-alpha, in an attempt to mask their helplessness.

The writer stares at the vacant page, the producer stares at the script, and searches for some formula to mask the terrifying fact: there's nobody here but me. That such a formula exists is an article of faith refuted by all our experience as writers, producers, and viewers. That we persist in its pursuit leads us into the most fascinating and silly of verbal games.

The Screenplay and the State Fair

It occurred to me that we were in the midst of a stock market boom.

First one and then another of my friends had mentioned this or that young person who'd increased the funds entrusted to them drastically, and I reflected that, with all this good fortune going on around, perhaps it would be a good idea for me to buy some stocks.

Slight further reflection suggested, however, that if knowledge of this boom had sufficient breadth and longevity to've come to my notice, the end could not be far off—that, in effect, my recognition (the first flush of greed, my call to "something for nothing") meant and must mean that the smart money was all through and it was time for the dumb money to pick up the tab.

Similarly with the screenplay. It is no longer an oddity, no longer a localized West Coast phenomenon, it is a fact of life that everyone has written his or her screenplay. The butcher, the baker, and their progeny have written a screenplay. I know, because they all have tried to get me to read them.

Then, if the modular, schematic nature of the Hollywood movie is clear to all, sufficiently clear that those daunted by the formal requirements of a thank-you note are essaying the thriller or romantic drama, must that not mean the end is at hand?

Yes.

The end of what? Of film as a dramatic medium.

For, certainly, these duffers, our friends the lawyers, doctors, and bus drivers, are not writing drama. They write, as do our betters in Hollywood, for gain, transforming this broad land into one large New Grub Street.

The urge of these acolytes is not dramatic but mercantile—to traduce all personal history, to subvert all perception or insight, into gain, or the hope of gain.

This work of writing the screenplay, then, is not an act of creation but an obeisance. It is a ceremony, a prostration, in which the individual's feelings and thoughts are offered to the golden calf: "There is no lie I will not tell, no secret I will not reveal, no treasure I will not debase, if you will just buy my screenplay."

Films themselves veer away from whatever residual taint of drama they may have had, and become celebrations of our mercantile essence, become, in effect, pure advertisement. This is especially true of The Summer Film.

The summer film is, first and last, a display of mercantile triumph—it is a display of technology.

Its attraction rests not on our desire for drama (the purpose of art being to conceal art) but on our desire for self-congratulation—on the display of technology per se.

Now, the highest achievement of American postindustrial achievement, the last best claim for American preeminence, is our technology. It is most handily displayed in the defense department and in the movies. In each we see the most shockingly novel rendition of the human capacity for elaboration.

The summer movie is not a drama, it is not even that admixture of drama and commerce, the Pageant; the summer movie is an Exhibition, pure and simple.

It is our State Fair, wherein the populace comes to be astonished, to gape at the new delights of commerce, and to be assaulted by advertisement.

The summer film has thrills and chills, as does its cousin the roller coaster.

It has the taint of the *louche,* as did its forebear the *nautch* show.

Rather than a midway lined by advertisement, the summer film is in itself an advertisement.

Yesterday's award of prizes, Cutest Baby and so on, has been supplanted by the announcement of the summer movie's grosses.

"Number One Film in the Country" replaces the broadcast of the winner of the greasy flagpole climb.

And the summer film has the exhibition of the prize farm animals—the film stars, coddled and petted and force-fed to such an extent that we must award them all our admiration.

The summer film, like the state fair, brings us together

and allows us the delight of shaking our head and saying to each other, "Will you get a load of *that?*"

If we reason or accept that this is not drama (which it is not) we need not decry the summer film's vapidity. It would be inappropriate to criticize the pie eating contest for lack of a reasonable respect for nutrition.

Drama, in the summer film, would be as out of place as landscape design in the fair's midway.

The screenplay bears the same relation to the drama that the bumf on the cereal box bears to literature. Its writing and its production are obeisance to the god of commerce.

The public pays its fine and spends its two hours in a celebration of waste in the time of abundance, the unambiguous enjoyment of the sun, the solstice festival, when worship of the antic god is all joy, and Nemesis is, for the moment, powerless.

In this druidical observance, she is, in fact, ritualistically murdered—the hero slays her at the conclusion of the film, and we go on our way, out into the friendly summer night.

Bad Boys

It was fashionable, in certain circles in the seventies and the eighties, to refer to men's supposed propensity to act in an uncaring, selfish, unfeeling, in short, "macho" way.

"Macho" meant bad.

Now, men, of course, *are*, by nature, arrogant, uncaring, and selfish.

And so are women.

It is a trick of the controlling person or organization to accuse the individual of those traits which are universal.

The manipulator describes these shortcomings as the particular fault of the accused.

Now, the truly arrogant, selfish individual is unconcerned with the opinion of others, and to him or her these accusations have no weight.

The non-arrogant individual, concerned at the presence or possibility of these unfortunate propensities in him- or herself, however, can be upset and/or controlled by accusations of arrogance and selfishness.

The pleas of various women's groups and various women for greater "emotional responsiveness" in men, the demand that men "listen," was not an emotional demand—no truly bruised sensibilities are saved by generalized behavior, only by specific redress. And "listen more" is a crypto-demand; it means "respond to that which I have not uttered."

The unuttered demand was for financial security.

It was not uttered as it was not consciously held. And the bitterness of much of the rhetoric and feelings of that time and on that issue came not from the inability of the "bad" men to respond to the demand "be more feeling" but from the repression of the thought "support me"—the anger engendered, again, not by the men but by the repression.

The amorphous demands—listen more, respond more, be more in touch with your own feelings—these demands can cause no reaction in the recipient but confusion, which confusion was greeted by the utterers as a proof of their original proposition: that men were/are, indeed, out of touch with their feelings.

In this interchange the utterer elects herself the parent and proposes to the man the role of the Bad Child. The bad, contentious, arrogant, out-of-touch child has failed in a way it cannot understand, but which is not only clear but of paramount importance to the parent.

As the child, by nature, both wants and needs to please, it needs to understand the reason for the parent's displeasure.

This mechanism allows the Bad Parent to manipulate the child at will, to cause confusion and, so, pain. And as the demands are incapable of being met, they engender in the child anger sufficient to, again, establish, both for him and for the parent, the truth of the original proposition.

The controlling mother acts in this way not to oppress the child, per se, but to dramatize, to act out a fantasy of control over those who oppressed *her*, her own bad parents.

The child, assigned the role of villain in this melodrama, is humiliated, angered, and confused.

No longer allowed to please, no longer rewarded for co-operation—in short, no longer loved—he embraces the role assigned to him as the sole way of pleasing (placating) his parents.

Opposition to their thesis does not free him from his parent's tyranny, and lays upon him the additional burden of guilt (as, above, his anger and resentment have proved to him his parent's point).

In subscribing to what he now considers a deserved mistreatment, the child lets himself be pressed into a constant state of reverie on the parent (the infant relies on the parent for sustenance and protection, the oppressed child for interpretation and for constant assurance of [withheld] love).

Now the Bad Parent has triumphed. The child is in thrall and dependent on the parent; and the overt oppression could cease, as control has shifted from the parent to the child's internalized "parental" voice—the child now torments himself.

But the oppression does *not* cease.

First, its cause is not present and so cannot be alleviated.

(The cause is, again, the parent's mistreatment by her own parents. Any attempt to rectify that situation or its ramifications must be made directly; it cannot be carried out by proxy. The cause of the Bad Parent's unhappiness lies in the past and must be so understood before it can be ameliorated.)

Secondly, the child now (and finally) *is* a failure. He now *is* out of touch with his feelings (now of rage) and their correct assignment; and he *has* let his parent down: he has failed to offer the solace, the redress, the absence of which has engendered the parent's unhappiness in the first place.

The child, assigned a role in the psychodrama he cannot understand, let alone resolve, can not respond to the parent's needs. He can only suffer.

Now, the then-fashionable demands—be more responsive, be more in touch with your feelings, be more in touch with your feminine side—were an act of repression; they were unconscious placeholders for an unacceptable thought. The thought caused anomie and was repressed, its repression caused anger, and the anger was expressed not at children but at those—as a group—similarly disposed to please (not a "mother figure" but *women*): heterosexual men.

(Now, this is not to say that heterosexual men are disposed to please women because they are altruistic, selfless, or "good" but simply that they have a disposition to please, if for no other reason than because women have something *they*, the men, want.)

Are *all* heterosexual men disposed, equally, to please women? No. But only those so disposed (and possessing a less than healthy ego) were capable of being brought under the control of the chimerical demand. (The others would simply respond to the irrational demand: "Oh, go away.")

What idea was repressed?

The clue lies, I think, in the unconscious choice of mechanism.

The utterer elects to "parentize" the recipient (to pay the recipient back for wrongs perpetrated on the utterer by her parents) and to make him, in his attempt to fulfill the unfulfillable, elect the utterer the center, the central arbiter of his world. She suggests by her actions that she is angry at being deprived of that benefit naturally and legitimately hers in childhood. She represses a desire for security, and an anger at security denied.

The middle-class woman entering the workforce in the seventies and eighties had, of course, to face prejudice against her as a woman.

She also, and, perhaps, as importantly, had to face that anomie, anxiety, and fear which confronts any man going out into the world; but she was not given the (I think meagre but, nonetheless, real) support offered by masculine tradition: "Yes. It's hard, but it *is* your job to make a living. That's how it's always been done, and what choice do you have?"

The middle-class woman faced the marketplace without that tradition at the same time she faced prejudice against her as a woman. And she found it legitimately frightening.

Her burden was further compounded by the pull of family versus job; so that, as oft noted, at work she felt guilty about abandoning her family, at home about forsaking her job.

This woman wanted someone to take care of her, to sort it out, and to offer her peace.

In this she was in the same position as her brethren down through history. But the woman's position was made more difficult by this: she had an out.

It was (and is) possible, theoretically and actually, for a woman *not* to go out into the workforce—to stay home as a housewife and/or mother.

And it was, I think, the pressure of this alternative which caused the creation of her oppressive (as incapable of being fulfilled) demands on men.

I think there are few men who, facing the adult world for the first time as an adult, have failed to fantasize about an exemption: "I think I'll just stay in bed; somehow my parents/society/the world will give me a pass, and I need not go into the world for which I know myself so singularly unprepared."

But for a woman such is—at least potentially—less of a fantasy.

She *might* stay home, *might* marry and live as a housewife. And if her milieu does not sanction such a solution, there are, she knows, milieux which do.

And so the well-nigh unbearable transition into unsupported individual life is mitigated by fantasy.

A woman might forsake (choose one or some) her desires, her philosophy, her friends, her ambition and, by so doing, spare herself pain.

But how, she asks, could a rational, *good* person consider it? (The man, by the way, asks himself the same question.)

In the eighties the financial times turned hard; the depression made jobs difficult to get and to keep. And women were the last into the workforce and the first out. There was a prejudice against them in any case, and many of them, being human, wished themselves well out of the terrifying fray.

A man cannot happily wish himself back to the childhood state; for in so doing he would deprive himself of male autonomy/integrity.

But the woman's (unconscious) state, again, offered her the (fictive or real—it was an *offer*) alternative of exemption and safety.

Hard times brought the wish to mind. The wish, to her, represented craven failure and was repressed. The repression caused anger, and the anger was directed against men.

Man had failed her. As a father he had bequeathed her an uncertain world. He had failed her as a husband—he was an ineffective breadwinner.

Both visions were unacceptable to the conscious mind. For each indicated a (again, universal) wish to be taken care of, which to the woman of the times equalled infantilization.

So they were repressed. But they found their expression in the mechanism of infantilization.

The attempt of infantilization of the male was caused by the wish to control the parent, to punish the parent. And the anger of the repressed wish grows hydraulically in response to the unacceptable nature of the thought: in this case, that the male is (if nothing else, in economic terms) the woman's better.

That the rhetoric of "machismo" and "expression of feelings" seems to have abated of late may be attributed both to an economic uptick and to the simple operation of time.

The women first charged with the responsibility of entering the workforce as absolute equals (for the benefit of both themselves and of their sisters) have gone on, for better or worse, with their careers.

Those who followed them entered a marketplace perhaps somewhat less antagonistic, but certainly less unknown.

The expectations, not only of women but of all Americans entering the workforce, have, of late, been lowered, and the new worker compares him- or herself and lot to that of their confused and disappointed parent, not, as that parent did, to the happier lot of a more financially and emotionally secure generation.

Resorts

My family and I were at a resort. My daughter held a papier-mâché ackee fruit. I wanted to photograph her with it so that one day I could say, "You see, here you are in the photograph, and here on your shelf is the same ackee fruit which has been in your room all this time." But could one not say that my vision of that future scene was, finally, just another excuse for a photograph, an attempt to fix in time something which would not be fixed—and so on ad infinitum, like the view of the two mirrors in the barber's chair, which reduces us to our first taste of existential nausea?

And what would she remember, in any case, of her trip at age fifteen months? Not the resort. Perhaps, as she grew older, she would remark on the juxtaposition of the black-and-white photo with the papier-mâché colored fruit and say of the trip, "That must have been the sort of people that my parents were—to wish me to remember this."

And so I fantasized about some future date, when I would be gone, and she would stare at the photograph, and I commiserated with myself, until I realized the sto-ical hint: "You will not have to bear Old Age. That man is being prepared now, by the gods."

And in what does this preparation consist save, for the most part, in forgetfulness? For me, my daughter, my wife, and the residents of that resort the week the East was being submerged by the blizzard of '96.

While for us it was Footprints on a Beach, and five-thirty mornings on the terrace. My daughter would sit on my lap, or we'd tour the place while her mother slept. We'd play the piano, "You Belong to Me," or perhaps "Frivolous Sal," and no one of the visitors would be up save us and one sour Brit sucking his cigarette and daring the rest of the world to wonder why his race never wash their hair.

My daughter and me.

When I was young, I did not tell her, my parents would take my sister and me to resorts in Wisconsin, in Tucson, in Miami Beach. I remember the smell of Noxema on my sun-burnt nose, and tincture of something-or-other on second-degree burns on my forearms, which burns kept me out of the pool. And the menu at Wolfie's, where, my father told me, Meyer Lansky was at his usual table in the corner.

I remember the flight to Miami from Chicago Midway. My family flew on the TWA Constellation, that beautiful dolphin of a plane, and stayed up all night and arrived at the hotel to eat grapefruit with the requisite cherry on top, and plead with the old folks to take us down to the pool.

I remember the plane rolling up to the terminal, and the skycaps loading the luggage out of the hold, onto the handcart, and then heaving it up into the silvered ramps in the claim area—a simple scene available only to memory or at the conclusion of Stanley Kubrick's *The Killing*.

I had occasion to come through the Miami airport just last week, after an absence of thirty-odd years, and found it somewhat changed. I was coming home from the eponymous resort of this article, with wife and infant child, and we had to change planes, retrieve our luggage, and proceed through customs and immigration, et cetera, and you're thinking, why is the chap whining, don't we all have to do the same?

And I respond, yes, indeed we do. As there are too many folk on the planet and I'm one of them, and so are you, but the only thing that that trip through the airport was more fun than was Knott's Berry Farm.

And I reflect on the whole Resort phenomenon. It seems to me that the spirit of regimentation is abroad in the land, and for all we might scoff at the Japanese, we Americans increasingly receive not delight and diversion but regimented distillation of the same in what we characterize as "our leisure time," a popular Yiddish rendition of which idea is "dance fast, the joint closes in an hour."

In the resort setting we ourselves are the cash crop, and we might understand the proprietor's vexation at idiosyncrasy—imagine a farmer having to deal with wheat which had an "attitude."

Yes, I have an attitude, I was born with one, and I spent much of our few days in the sun wondering if, on balance, I'd have been happier with New York's snow-bound squalor than the knowledge that Tuesday was Beach Party Night.

I am a crybaby, and my wife straightened me up on the

third day: "You aren't here to enjoy yourself," she said, "you're here to relax."

I could attribute my inability to enjoy resorts to my being a Jew, and the prized theory/observation (prized, at the very least, by me) that we Jews do not travel well (see: Exodus), but I spent a bit of my youth, as I've said, at resorts, and at Jewish resorts at that. (In the fifties, resorts were classified into Jewish and Restricted, meaning No Hebrews Need Apply.)

The Wisconsin resorts of my youth were the equivalent of the Catskills for us Chicago Jews. I loved the free pinball games and the "activities": Simon says, and the shuffle-board, and the dressing up—the Kamp Kare-Free attitude, in short.

One year my father announced we were not going to return to our resort. When pressed for an explanation, gave out with, "Too many Jews." I am sure the alternative destinations, as he sampled them, were punishment enough for his decision. At least I so mused in my recent trip.

I felt the folks at our (current) resort to be standoffish; and I am, quite sufficiently standoffish for all of us, thank you very much.

We were told "they" had been coming down to the Caribbean, to this current joint, for years and years, had contracted and dissolved both liaisons and alliances there, came down with children, made lifelong friends, and gossiped with the regulars about the interloper swine who were, finally, just trying to get their family out of a snowstorm.

This information about gossiping I found charming, as my family and I (Fair-Game Newcomers) have no charac-

teristics sufficiently noticeable and underbred to engender speculation.

And who were these gossipers, I ask, but run-of-the-mill
middle-class Americans come down to the Caribbean to get
some sun, and be fussed to death, and gossip about their
betters? Perhaps I am still expiating my father's sin.

And, truth be told, I *am* that Jew he was avoiding (as
was he). And, while preferring solitude, will take shuffle-
board over golf and tennis any day.

I remember Miami Beach in the fifties and the opening of
the Fontainebleau, Eden Roc, Nautilus Hotel—all of which
openings I, in my mind's eyes, seem to remember attending.

I was absolutely at the opening of the Nautilus Hotel
back in the fifties.

The nuclear submarine *Nautilus* had just been commis-
sioned. Its crew was invited to the congruent ceremony
at the hotel. I remember many of them arrayed, in their
whites, up the ladder to the high diving board and out
onto the board itself, where one sailor, at the most appo-
site moment of jollity, fell into the pool.

Latterly I met a man who had been part of that *Nautilus*
crew, and I asked after the fellow who fell in the pool. I was,
of course, hoping against hope that the man would respond, "Hell, that was *me*," but he did not; and he didn't recall the man, the pool, or the hotel, and he told me that, as a
member of that crew, if it had happened, he'd have been
there and if he'd been there, he'd have remembered it.

I wrote off his lapse as the gods preparing him (or perhaps me) to bear old age. And went upon my way.

What would it have meant had he responded, "I was that
man who fell into the pool?"

Whose life would it have made easier, whose burden lighter, and who am I to wish the forces that be to bend their overtaxed attention to my silly request for a moment of cheap coincidence?

And so what if the ackee in the photograph is that same yellow and red ackee right there on the shelf? Mightn't we say that (*pace* photo-aesthetes) the ability to record something which had actually occurred is the point of the exercise?

But I digress, and will tax your good graces back to a resort, once again, in Wisconsin, and a talent show.

I was seven or eight, and that would make my sister four or five. We had been press-ganged by our parents to perform. I was to sing "Young at Heart," lately made popular by Frank Sinatra, and she was to sing along. Or she was to sing and I to play it on the piano, or some such countdown to disaster.

Sure as shooting, there we were, terrified, showing-away for the evening adult crowd, and after three or four bars she began to cry, and the audience to laugh at her.

I did, I believe, a creditable "Stop the music!" and stood down-in-one and lambasted the crowd to contrition. An early example of noble selflessness, the continuation of which has been a trifle piebald, but if I escape the fiery furnace at the end, perhaps I can thank Frank Sinatra, and how many can say the same?

I recall a resort called Starved Rock Lodge in Illinois somewhere (to us Chicagoans "Illinois" exists only as a placeholder between the postal designation "Chicago" and the zip code).

It was an Indianated affair, the Midwest rendition of the

East's Niagara—a honeymoon resort named for that noble and, it would seem, fairly quotidian Indian Act of Love Suicide to which, as Mr. Twain reminds us, the hotelier owes so much.

I recall vast lodge beams and Beacon blankets, and a pre-adolescent sense of the theatricality of the whole damn thing.

And I recall Adirondack resorts in the seventies—all fallen on hard times and stinking of a hundred years of mice and bad food. I recall corridors like Coleridge's "cavern's mea-sureless to man," and it strikes me that *that* ditty was itself an ode to a resort and that *his* opium dream of pleasure was destroyed by the advent of one too many visitors—much in the same way that my group and *their* group irked each other in this last Caribbean excursion.

The *reductio ad absurdum* of the Resort Experience, i.e., the industrial masquerading as the sybaritic, is the Miami Airport.

It shares with the theme park the hours of cramped wait-ing and the anxiety about one's young; and worries over customs, immigration, and baggage, while not quite the "thrill" of the park's rides, do have the merit of being unpre-dictable.

I got to the passport desk and was trembling like a leaf, sen-sitive creature that I am. The line was vast and the press of re-turnees a glimpse of hell. But I had made it to the front of the line, my family with me. The mass of humanity was waved through immigration, just a glance at their passports. But the officer kept me on for a second and then a third glance and some questions—I recalled, later, I was trembling, which would bring the blood to such an officer's cheeks.

The experience of the airport had taken the starch out of me, but, being in order, after everything was said and done, we passed through into that section of the airport which was the United States.

I reflected, that evening, I had missed that most lovely moment of the Trip Abroad—the loveliest moment, alas, of the resort experience also—when the Customs officer hands back your passport and says, "Welcome home."

Noach

Let us suppose, as Freud suggests, that there is the *manifest* dream, the dream we remember, and there is the *latent* dream—the dream the manifest dream is constructed to obscure, the dream we would rather forget, which is too powerful, too upsetting, too unsettling.

The memory/dream of infant sacrifice becomes cleansed into the binding of Isaac; the memory of infanticide becomes Moses' shattering of the tablets.

The second, or prettier, dream in the Noach story is the Tower of Babel.

Human beings, the story informs us, when they associate into large groups, inevitably set about mischief; they are susceptible to outward and inward exhortations to idolatry, that is, to self-worship. They reason or intuit that if one person is powerful, the group must be geometrically more powerful of arm, reason, intellect—that given a large enough

up, nothing is impossible. We see such an error in the
wer of Babel, and in its most modern rendition, the Infor-
1ation Superhighway, and, in fact, in all of human history
in between. Banding together into large groups leads to idolatry, folly, and destruction. Manifest Destiny, the Monroe
Doctrine, the Gulf of Tonkin Resolution, the House Un-
American Activities Committee—in these we can see, from a
remove, the very exuberance engendered by solidarity as a
tool diagnostic of arrogance and the inevitable cruelty to
which it leads. America First, the Horst Wessel Lied, Desert
Storm—the self-assured, fervent communal activity allows
us to submerge ourselves and our conscience, to lay down
the burden of uncertainty, to disregard the ambiguous and
the difficult. We can and do characterize this happiness as
"being made whole," but the Torah tells us we should be
warned that "being made whole" by a sense of our own
power is not a healthy state, it is idolatry, and leads directly
to grief.

Our American wonder at having saved the world in 1945,
our efforts to prolong that feeling, led to Vietnam, to
Korea, to Desert Storm, to a country debased and impov-
erished by the defense establishment, and the necessity of
a constant Evil Oppressor.

"Do not band together into Large groups; you will do
Evil." This is the *manifest* dream. It is clear, it is logical, it
is, in effect, a straightforward morality tale: "In Situation
A do not act as these characters do, or, as you see, an unfortunate result will ensue."

That is the Tower of Babel, but the Tower story is the
manifest, the scrambled, the encrypted/cleansed, version
of a previous *latent* dream, which it attempts to master

through repetition. And the latent dream is not a cautionary tale, it is a straight-out horror.

"You have been sinning, and I, HaShem, repent me of having made the World, and I will destroy it. And the waters prevailed, and all the high mountains that were under the heavens were covered, and all HaShem had made was obliterated."

In fact, the waters rose to fifteen cubits *above* the high mountains, "and all in whose nostrils was the breath of life, of all that were on dry land, died."

In the primary dream, the latent dream, the Flood, HaShem saw that the wickedness of man was very great and that all imagination and every thought of his heart was only evil continually. *Rak rah col ha'yom.* No repentance is possible; all are destroyed, as all are evil.

But Noach, we are told, found grace in the eyes of the Lord.

But Freud said that just as the manifest hides the latent dream, so the latent dream conceals a primal, infantile trauma. And we might suggest that the height of the waters, fifteen cubits *over* the mountains, is a clue that the flood deals with a *further* submerged memory, that the waters rise not only sufficiently to obliterate all life, but to a height sufficient to make any attempt at retrospection bootless. The Land (the Old Life) can not even be discerned (remembered).

Why?

I believe that the story is about the wish to kill, that the world-destruction dream, "Every thing was killed in the flood," hides the fury-rage-anger of the primitive-infantile idea: I wish to destroy the world; I have been angered and wish to kill not only those who anger me but *everyone.* My anger (so reasons the infant mind) is all-powerful as *I* am all-powerful. I do not need an excuse; I, myself, am the occasion. What could be better than to kill?

"And it came to pass when men began to multiply on the face of the Earth daughters were born to them, that the sons of God saw the daughters of men, that they were fair, and they took themselves wives of all whom they chose and there were giants in the Earth."

Who were these giants? The parents. Why is the writer wroth? He/she wants to be the sole object of the giants' attention and cannot compete with the attraction of adult sexuality and, so, wants the Earth to be destroyed.

So the double-encrypted wish-dream in the Noach story is the memory of the desire to renounce/forget murder. And, once again, we have the psychological cauldron of the Second Son who inverts his hatred of the elder brother (and perhaps his guilt at survival of ritual sacrifice) and projects the guilt as the desire of the older brother to kill *him*. What must the child feel, what must the infant feel, what must the race feel which grew up in a culture practicing infant sacrifice? The unformed mind there saw its wildest and most cherished fantasies enacted and endorsed, and devoted itself to the creation of an idol which would require and endorse such actions and, so, relieve the individual of guilt: e.g., Baal, godless Communism, Peace in Our Time, the American Way, the Revolution...

That one can not have what one wants—world dominion, infallibility, boundless wealth—that one *should* not have what one wants, that idolatry is a destructive, infantile state the tropism toward which must be superseded, is the message of Noach. The message of the Torah is that though we conquer our lower nature once, and at the beginning, and again and again, it will reassert itself, for that's what it is to be human. The clean and the unclean animals will be on the ark, the sons of Noach will begin to build the tower at the conclusion of the Begats, and though the world be submerged and the mountains be covered to the depth of fifteen cubits, the Torah time and again and continually informs us that there is a story beneath the story and that the very fact of its encryption should compel our interest and study.

The Fireman's Child

We search for that to which we may enslave ourselves:
we may choose a machine (the computer); we may choose
a human being (a dictator), or a supposedly perfect human
mechanism (a law or a fundamentalist religion or an organization), and call it divine and beyond possibility of error.
Our subjugation to this person, organization, or idea,
however it might prove painful, destructive, or absurd, we
call the highest reason.

We know that any one legislator must be hypocritical
and, not improbably, act in a venal, criminal, or questionable manner (just as any other citizen), but we feel that
agglomeration somehow improves—nay, cleanses; nay,
purifies—the legislator, rendering the legislative body a
group of demigods of probity, perception, and grace.

A fireman and his wife adopted a boy.

They had contracted with his birth mother, a single

woman who did not wish or was not able to raise the child.

The adoptive family raised the boy from birth.

When he turned four, a man appeared who claimed and was proved to be the boy's biologic father. He had been the lover of the birth mother. They had separated before the man knew of her pregnancy. On learning now, almost five years later, of the child's existence, he sued for custody, and the court awarded it to him.

The boy was taken, by court order, from a loving, secure home, the only home he had ever known, from adoring parents and siblings, and awarded in custody to a man he had never seen.

There exists photographs and videotapes of the child being taken, screaming, from his home, his fingers pried from the only mother he would ever know.

In the background we see sheriff's deputies, several of them with their faces buried in their hands.

The decision outraged reason, justice, human concern for the child, and community sentiment. Its rectitude resided only in the mind of the judge, who saw the law as something other than human (that is, as perfect); who sought, in a difficult case, to excuse his confusion or cowardice through adherence to the supposed principals of that mechanism his actions reduced to absurdity.

But what would I have done had I been a member of that crowd, or had I been that neighbor who pried the child's fingers from his mother?

For the mechanism did not exist—

To say "stop" would have required, on the part of the neighbor, of a deputy, of an onlooker, an act of vast heroism.

For they could not have imagined, in that heat of passion—nor, indeed, can I at this safe remove—how such an act of defiance could have come to any healthy, happy, or positive end. And that is, of course, the greatest heroism; to perform an act for its own sake because it is right, because the actor knows—not in reference to an authorized source but in the absence of any such reference—that the act is right.

How can the individual differentiate between this knowledge, leading to heroism, and that consciousness of mission which results in destruction and outrage?

Perhaps the true act of heroism is one of submission, rather than of assault; as, in the case of the child, the essence of the heroic act would have been to *side with* him.

With such an intention the component of *resistance to authority* would have been small, the essential act being one of *surrender*, of, in effect, confession of powerlessness in the face of human error. And thus, finally, of humility before God.

In the Simpson case we see applauded *subjugation to the will of the state,* where those unhappy with the verdict attempt to rationalize away their confusion or dissatisfaction thusly: "The state is superior. And its laws are just. We cannot, as individuals, know Right until it has been passed through some engine of abstraction."

The individual's sense of security is, in this case, determined by his ability to accept the absurd as being the workings of an intellect greater than his own; or, at the least, a—in the instance in question—lamentable application of a principle the protection of which is of such importance that subscription to momentary cruelty or nonsense in its name is not only necessary but in fact praiseworthy.

How can there be independent action without independent thought? How can there be independent thought in the face of the screaming demands for conformity, and unanimity of the mass culture?

Were we to destroy all mass communication and disband the schools, could the result be a civilization any more pagan, superstitious, and preliterate than that in which we live?

The case of the fireman's child was an example of that savagery of which the Torah came into being to mark the end—infant sacrifice as the approved action of the ignorant in the face of the unknowable.

Poor But Happy

"We were poor, but so was everybody else, so we didn't know we were poor."

We hear the phrase and impute to the speaker a happy childhood. We understand the speaker was happy as he or she was the member of a *group*.

Eric Hoffer wrote that in countries where there is freedom, everyone demands equality; and much of American social intercourse is an attempt to forcibly create a common social and ethical milieu.

Polling and talk shows—both institutionalized gossip—hold down one end of the spectrum at the other end of which we find the militia movement and bombings.

Because we find uncertainty intolerable. The first question an American asks a stranger with whom he or she will be spending more than a few moments is "What do you do?"

This means "How can I understand you, *class* you, determine your worth? Are you a member of my group?"

Here is a more egregious question: The American Jew is asked, "Are you a Jew or an American first?"

What an impertinence. By what possible license is it asked?

For the hearer even to entertain it is to ascribe to a supposed right or prerogative of the majority culture—not to determine the hearer's position but to assert the speaker's right over him or her.

To consider responding to the question is as to consider it one's duty to explain away anti-Semitism—like the rape victim responding, "Alright, let me *see* if I can remember how short a skirt I *was* wearing that day."

To endorse the majority culture's arrogant behavior is to collude in race hatred.

The phrases "I am a Jew, but I am not a practicing Jew," "I am a Jew culturally but not religiously," "My parents were Jews, but I am not a Jew," "I am a Jew, but I disagree with the conduct of Israel," et cetera—these phrases, while uttered as a declaration of autonomy, are, to the contrary, a ritual of subjugation to the dominant culture.

It is not that the positions enumerated above are illegitimate but that their *broadcast* is, quite literally, egregious: it is placing oneself outside the group. And whose business is it? How can it possibly be the prerogative of the dominant culture to request information on the extent and nature of your alliance? And why would a content individual unilaterally vouchsafe same?

The phrases "I am a Jew but . . . ," et cetera, mean, "Don't despise me. I, too, see something unlovely in my race, culture, religion. I am just like you."

But there is nothing unlovely about our people or practices, there is only internalized self-hatred.

What causes anti-Semitism? What causes race hatred? It is caused by self-loathing. The deranged individual or culture, the oppressor, cannot bear the knowledge of his or her own worthlessness and, so, projects the hated qualities onto a group easily identified as the Other. The only other necessary factor is that the group elected must be seen as powerless.

Can one change a bigot's perceptions? No. More to the point, perceptions are not the cause of racial hatred. It is the very gap between the perception of the bigot and the reality of the situation which intensifies race hatred, for as the bigot's acts become more cruel, his (for the first time, real) knowledge of his own worthlessness grows; and from this now-increased sense of "bad," he becomes more cruel and ascribes his escalated behavior to "proofs" of the victim's worthlessness. For example: The Jews are bad. Let us oppress them. They don't fight back. The Jews are *weak* and bad.

There is no peace to be found in siding with the bigot. The thought "Well, let it slide," awakes an ongoing internal dialogue: "Should I have spoken out?" "What would I have hoped to have accomplished?" "It wouldn't have changed anything." "It was a minor, and perhaps an *unintended,* slight." This doesn't sound like peace to me.

The only peace—and I think we Jews have excellent models in other minority communities—the only peace,

if one is a Jew, is to be a member of the tribe and to re-
sent deprecation of it (others *and* one's own), just as one
would of one's family.

I don't mean that bigots should be resented or responded
to with anger, with aggression, or with the intent to "bring
about a change," or even to "influence."

The anti-Semitic slight should be responded to not for the
sake of the bigot but for the sake of the recipient Jew—to
proclaim and, so, to enjoy one's membership in the group.

Brompton Cocktail

*World War II: A mixture of various drugs
administered as euthanasia*

Jafsie

A schoolmarmish fellow in Brooklyn told Lindbergh he
believed he could be of use in locating his kidnapped son.

The fellow, John F. Condon, gained Lindbergh's ear, and
his confidence, and, in fact, accompanied him to the rendezvous where the ransom was to be exchanged for the
child.

Who was this fellow?

He invited all to call him by his nickname, Jafsie, an
acronym of his initials JFC.

Bruno Richard Hauptmann was arrested and charged
with the kidnapping and murder of the Lindbergh baby.

The case against him was weak in the extreme. Some of
the ransom money was found in his house.

He explained he had been asked to hold it by one Isidore Fisch, a sometime associate, who had since died.

And there was much exculpatory evidence. Hauptmann asserted he had been at work on a construction crew at the time of the kidnapping.

There was a time sheet at the job site. The page concerning the day in question had been defaced.

A homemade ladder was used to gain access to the Lindbergh child's room.

Wood in the ladder was somehow supposed to match, in grain, porosity, and other various particulars, wood in the flooring of Hauptmann's attic—to match it so exactly as to exclude possibility of error.

Hauptmann, a skilled craftsman, was confronted with the slapdash, skewed ladder at the trial and asked if he had built it.

"I am a carpenter," he responded.

At the trial Lindbergh and Condon identified Hauptmann's voice as that of the kidnapper whom they had heard, two years before, shout, "Hey, over here." And that was the evidence which convicted Hauptmann.

He went to the electric chair asserting his innocence.

Hauptmann was a man, it seems, who was in the wrong place at the wrong time.

But who and what was Condon?

It is somewhere between possible and likely that he was one of the conspirators.

And if I cast myself into the fantasy of the event, the screaming, unremembered nightmare, the blaring repressed element which informs the kidnapping is "Who was Condon?" Which leads to the more basic question, a question perhaps more important, as more deeply repressed, "Why was it unimportant to the concerned to know?"

Why do we accept the vicious and ludicrous—the blood libel, the domino theory, the idea of un-American activities?

Why do we say of the polarity of common sense observation and vicious enormity, "Well, the truth most probably lies somewhere in between?"

Over dinner one night someone mentioned the Albigensian Crusade.

How Simon de Montfort broke his journey in Avignon and found it good, while there, to exterminate the city's Jews.

There was a woman at dinner I had known for thirty years, foreign-born, raised in Europe, multilingual, cultured.

"Well," she said of the murdered Jews, "I'm sure to a certain extent they brought it on themselves."

"How was that?" I asked.

"They flaunted their wealth," she replied.

I spoke through my amazement and inquired how the Poor Jews there had brought it on themselves and, then, how it was that the rich non-Jews had not.

She was silent. The refutation of her vicious folly gave rise not to understanding but to a rage which only confirmed and augmented her prejudice.

I believe we are a savage species, that we evolved to hunt, and that our evolutionary tools, intelligence, and the grasping hand, combined (inevitably, in a hunter) into a genius for weapons and, so, into a genius *and a necessity* for identifying the prey and the enemies on which those weapons must be used.

The beaver cuts down trees to ease a hurtful itching in its gums. If it does not gnaw wood it is driven mad.

The logs being down, the beaver finds a use for them.

We happily trust our reason to bring us to the Truth (by which we mean a blameless state).

The interesting notion that we are equipped to recognize, let alone utilize Truth, frees us to override the nagging influence of conscience—for our reason leads us not toward godliness but toward the most efficient use of our capacity to dominate.

Now, in our folly, we devote our day to toying with and speculating about machines which can do nothing other than *keep track.* We call this employment of our time common sense.

In the last stages of the miser's dementia we stack and restack and convert or rearrange our wealth. The miser calls it coin, we call it information; both mean a world completely subdued to our hand.

Like the miser, we lock ourselves alone in our room and call it joy and wisdom.

Perhaps, having to our satisfaction perverted the natural world, we are directed to subdue our own capacity, to sit drugged, alone and dying, and wait for that Kindly Old Man, the yearned-for guest of the hopeless, to wait for death. Jafsie was the Angel of Death.

John Henry

I am a child of the first generation of the atomic age.

We were raised under—it seemed to us, at any rate—the very real possibility of nuclear war.

The machinery of air-raid warning and drills was in place from the Second World War; and our parents, who had just lived through that war, were, in the main, the wrong audience to consider our stunned outrage at that which, to us, was a new reality.

Wait one moment, I remember thinking, the world may be ended in the next moment—everything we know may be blown away by the push of a button—and yet you can continue one moment to the next as if that were not so? In my age and milieu we were stunned by my parents' generation's acceptance of the inevitability of war.

I spent much time and energy in my thirties brooding about imminent destruction, and the meaning of a species which could maneuver itself into such a corner.

My search for philosophy induced me to accept—if only hypothetically—the idea that what seemed to be a problem was, perhaps, a solution.

Perhaps, I reasoned, nuclear destruction was a naturally evolved mechanism for doing away with a pesky problem. (The problem, in my more sanguine moments, was named "overpopulation" and in my less, "genus *Homo*".)

Perhaps, I thought, the global organism, just like the individual body, employs strategies to fight disease, to restore equilibrium; and, again, just as in the individual body, sometimes those strategies are themselves destructive.

Perhaps, just as the fever comes into being to fight infection, and the fever itself kills, so nuclear war, et cetera.

Now all of this was in part at least a handy identification of general and less general adolescent and young adult anxieties. And part was the continued astonishment at horror.

Time, of course, and use, dulled my apprehensions, as they had those of my parents; and I came, like them, to consider many an enormity of sufficient longevity reasonable, or, at least, explicable. Or, at least, theoretically explicable, were one only in possession of "all the facts."

As the threat of nuclear destruction faded (or, better put, as faded my apprehension of the same), I granted its embellishment—my theory of global-holocaust-as-euthanasia—a rest.

But I have lately revived it.

The fable is the epigram for John O'Hara's *Appointment in Samarra*. The man was in the marketplace, in Basra; he saw the Old Woman Who Was Death, and she threw up her arms to grab him.

He fled by the swiftest horse to Samarra.

As he dismounted, the Old Woman Who Was Death grasped him to her.

The man asked why she had not grabbed him that morning when she raised her arms to him. She replied she raised her arms not to arrest him but in astonishment. She was astonished to see him in Basra, as she knew she had an appointment with him in Samarra.

And just as I was a child of the first generation of the atomic age, so, equally, was I of the first generation of television.

How can we, if we retreat just a bit, explain to ourselves this destructive toy?

We say that it can do all things, much as the drug addict knows that life without drugs is meaningless.

We are addicted to its flickering lines, and go to any length to explain our addiction. We call it the desire for entertainment, for information, for education, for "connection."

We are on the cusp or beyond the cusp of the moment when the television-computer becomes the focus of our lives—the fireplace, the book, the school, the mart, the stage, the drawing tablet, the workplace.

It proliferates in the service of death, offering ever more elaborate and useless variations and renditions to lure us to its worship.

And I think that the true meaning of the blithely bandied term "information" is oblivion, that it is the television, and not the atomic bomb, which will destroy civilization, that our destiny, as the poet predicted, was never the bang but was the whimper, and that this ludicrously contrarian essay and its like are that whimper's component.

John Henry celebrates the victory of a workman over a mechanical steam drill. John Henry is the strongest man on the mountain. He is outraged when the boss wants to replace him with a mechanical device. He tests himself against the machine, wins, and dies.

As a youth in the hootenanny days, I wondered at the song. I thought it hypocritical to celebrate John Henry's victory, for, surely, the *next* man couldn't beat the steam drill—John Henry himself couldn't beat it over a protracted period, and no one would be able to vanquish the next generation of the machine—and, so, our celebration of him was disingenuous.

But, of course, the meaning of the song was not that he won but that he died—that the one person capable of defeating the machine is no more. The song, seemingly a paean to resistance, is, I think, more an assertion of its use-lessness—"The hero died in the attempts; what do you think *you* could do?"

The film *Independence Day* features a monstrous space-craft which comes to destroy us. It hovers over our cities and opens a curious circular orifice in its midst, and from that orifice comes the death-ray, or whatever it is.

The audience cheers the *pro forma* victory of the Earth-lings at the end (the President marshals a group of stal-warts from around the world and leads them to victory, flying the alien plane itself); but I think the film's popu-larity is due to the grateful vision of the spacecraft.

It squats, its anus opens, and it shits on our life.

This is, I think, a handy inversion of the less acceptable underlying statement of the film: our life (our cities) *is* shit, is beyond repair, and we would *welcome* that force which would destroy it.

The space creatures in this movie, as in most of the genre, have come to our world as they have depleted their own. They have ruined their nest and have come to drive us from ours.

They are, of course, as any monsters, projections of our-selves.

It is *we* who have ruined our nest, and the alien inva-sion theme satisfies because it is a confession.

In our befouled nest we search for solace, distraction, justification, anesthesia, and find them all in the televi-sion-computer.

It is not, we say, that we are drugged, without occupation, without community, without hope, illiterate and without will; we are informing ourselves—the machine will enable us to write better, to draw better, to communicate better, to add, to shop, to sell, to buy, to court.

Nothing will make it go away.

It is not just a part of our culture, it is our culture.

It is not that "the machine can do anything," it is that in accepting the machine we accept the limits of its operations as "everything that we might want to do."

It does not tell us what people *think*, it tells us what people tell the machine that they think—or, more accurately, what some person very possibly possessed of a private agenda wishes to tell us that people have told the machine they think.

The machine does not tell us about the nature of the world, it tells us what that person programming the machine wishes to tell us about the nature of the world.

Is it possible that this "information"might be entered in the machine altruistically, or, at least, impartially?

It is—if not actually, then presently—impossible. For the machine is a television and the power of television to immobilize has and will *always* be exploited by those attempting to control.

That control is now passing from the commercial to the political; the two are merging, or have merged.

Mid-century literature envisioned an anthropomorphic machine which would do all our bidding. It was called a robot, and we looked on it as an entertaining misrepresentation both of the purpose and of the powers of science.

But here we are at the century's end, and the machine has been developed.

It is immobile and sends *us* to do its bidding.

It is inevitable that the computer become the tool of

censorship and enslavement. It is already functioning in that way in the service of consumerism.

There is only an accidental and, I think, a momentary difference of extent between censoring those items of information deemed marginal, unentertaining, inaccurate, et cetera, and censoring those items deemed "productive of public discord."

I can envision no device more capable of spreading ignorance and illiteracy than the computer.

It is, I think, like the atom bomb, a naturally evolved engine of oblivion, a sign, like the Tower of Babel, that the civilization has run its course.

Why Don't You Write
with a Computer?

We children in the 1950s had a clear view of both the form and function of the robot. It would be a more or less anthropomorphic machine, and it would relieve us of the more menial tasks, leaving us free to do the thinking.

The reality seems to be, rather, the unfortunate reverse, and we find ourselves the hewers of wood and the drawers of water for the machine.

Use of the computer, stocked with forms and self-correcting as to spelling and grammar, makes us illiterate, much as television's mindless and interminable banality has made us stupid—unable to recognize, let alone understand, the simplest human interactions.

The automobile separated us from our neighbors so that our brief interactions occur not with those with whom we share interests, concerns, or beliefs but with salespeople, and we have, in short, become the robot—programmed by our machines to spend our leisure hours entranced by advertisement, our vacations waiting in various lines, our work lives punching buttons.

The question "Why don't you write with a computer?" is not a request for information but a political demand. In tone and force it is akin to "Why aren't you displaying the flag on this, the Fourth of July?"

It is, as any rhetorical question, essentially an attack from cover, a demand that the writer submit to a universally acknowledged good, and the questioner acts as a duly constituted representative of authority/tyranny.

For the identification with the robot/machine is the wish to immerse oneself in the mass, to avail oneself of the most popular wisdom, and, so, to put anxiety at rest.

"Why don't you use a computer?" is, in form, the Inquisition's "Why don't I find pork in your home?"

The absence of pork, the absence of the American flag, the reluctance or unwillingness of the individual to justify before the House Un-American Activities Committee ("Why would you be reluctant to testify if you have nothing to hide?") are *prima facie* evidence of the accused's guilt. For the crime, in a fascist system, is the unwillingness to subscribe to the nonsensical.

The lack of linkage to and dependence upon the machine is increasingly being understood as an affront to the Body Politic. The country is governed now not by men and women of principle, of common sense, or even of decided, if self-interested, views. The country is governed by strivers who claim the right to act upon the statistical data the machine vouchsafes them.

Consider Newt Gingrich's suggestion that the plight of

the underprivileged would be ameliorated by putting a computer onto every ghetto schoolroom desk.

This was the occasion of mirth on the part of his detractors.

They saw it as an inept, untutored, and disingenuous attempt to suggest social improvement.

But perhaps his suggestion reveals a deeper, an unconscious, understanding of the role of the machine.

What did he want from the poor, and what possible good could their use of the computer do for him? It could get the poor to shut up.

Race Driving School

The thing of it is, as they say, that there is no help for it. It is like being discovered at the remote resort with a woman one-third one's age. "Yes," you might try to explain, "she is my niece," or some other such dodge. Upon reflection, however, it might seem the gaffe was not the tryst but the lame alibi.

Similarly, in the classroom at the driving school, there we were, twelve gents who, taken singularly, might have personified stability, substantiality, or bluffly healthy middle age. In toto, however, we were a roomful of old farts.

Like the gent with his niece, it became crystal clear upon rendition of the alibi.

"Say your name and what brings you here," the instructor said.

"Blah blah, and my wife-son-son-in-law-partner sent me here for my fortieth-fiftieth-sixtieth birthday," each replied. Oh lord.

All honor, therefore, to the instructors. They explained and re-explained the essentials of race driving. We had several blackboard hours' worth of the physics and geometry of the automobile, et cetera, but, significantly, they put up with an ongoing recital of the worst excuse for conversation I have ever heard in my life.

For we wannabes, having been at least moderately successful in our nonracing lives, were each accustomed to "lead," that is, to make bad jokes in aid of some mutual endeavor, our ignorance of the mechanics of which endeavor induced us to believe that all that was lacking for its success was the application of our personality.

But this was not a mutual endeavor, and we were, here, not captains (or subalterns) of industry, not doctors, but students, and not only were we regressed, but we were frightened. At least I was.

We were going to drive these cunning little formula cars around the track at high speeds, and in a manner to which we were unaccustomed; and, to make matters worse, it was pissing down rain.

My theory of aerodynamic equanimity holds that one does not have to get upset until the stewardess does.

Here the theory was of no use, as the instructors, far from being upset, seemed thrilled, and this made my anxiety worse.

But let me address the mechanics of instruction.

I once was exposed to transcendental meditation, and

found, at the risk of blowing the gaff, that the instructors' (completely effective) method consisted of self-suggestion. One sat in a room and listened, for, I believe, several evenings, to a chap drone on about the benefits and history of the technique. Nothing was said about its mechanics, or the method by which one would learn the same; the fellow just went on with a bunch of "bumf."

On the long-awaited night of Initiation, one met with the instructor, did a bit of nonspecific folderol with ritual objects, and then found oneself, as if by magic, in that previously unknown state the mysterious existence of which induced one to sign up in the first place. Stunningly good.

Now, at the driving school, the curriculum was chopped up thus: First, chalk talks outlining the maneuver; then, the class splits into two groups: one group gets into the cars and attempts to employ the teaching, the other group retires to a convenient height in the infield and watches Group One's triumphs and miscalculations. Groups One and Two then shift.

Terrific design, for, watching, one says both "Hell, *I* get it" and "Hell, *I* can do better than that." And then, performing, one is self-exhorted-shamed-challenged to make good and repair one's overarching arrogance.

T. E. Lawrence wrote that he thought men go to war because the women are watching.

I know he knew something of war, but it is generally acknowledged that he knew nothing whatever about women, and, I believe, we must excuse his pretty but incorrect pronouncement. Men go to war because the men are watching.

And that's why we went faster around the track.

Much of it has to do with overcoming fear. And I believe that is a great lesson, like the great lesson of boxing: to get hurt is not the same as to get killed.

After a few circuits on the track, practicing rudiments, it becomes clear that, at least during the proceedings of the school, there is little or no danger—the track is bounded in the main by flat fields, and should one spin out (as happens to most of us at one time) one simply drives back out of the field and onto the track.

We are given simple, mechanical instructions: brake at that cone, begin your turn at the next cone, look where you want to go.

(This I found particularly useful. Our instructor said that we'd all heard that to get out of a skid one "steers into the skid" but that, on reflection, this instruction doesn't mean much of anything. The way to get out of the skid, he said, was simply to *look* where one wanted to go. The hands, he explained, have no brains, they only do what is required of them. Most people in an accident, he said, report that the last thing they saw before the crash was the thing they hit. Because they were looking at it; the hands steered the car to it.

It is the most valuable lesson, to me, of the school, to, rather, look where one wants the car to go. I like it so much I might actually elaborate it into a universal [or greeting card] axiom.)

Before my time at the driving school, I'd spent several days unwinding at a spa.

On the walls of the spa were various feel-good sentiments aspiring to philosophy.

One was: A SHIP IS SAFE IN HARBOR, BUT THAT'S NOT WHAT A SHIP IS FOR. I liked this one. If not immediately employable, it, at least, is punchy.

Of my other linguistic treats at the spa, the first featured two middle-aged ladies in jogging gear. I was walking behind them on the way to chow, and one commented: "I like my sharp pain." Not being averse to revelations of the curious, I followed close behind. Her companion nodded and then leaned in to respond with what I hoped would be her own confession of inversion, enormity, or deviation. "Well, yes," she said, "many people like the shar-pei, but I prefer my golden."

The second experience occurred at breakfast. I was seated next to a man my devotion to accountability in journalism compels me to describe as a "geezer." He was sitting, staring at the table before him.

He looked up at me as I sat. "I'm having conflicts," he said. I was touched but affronted he'd chosen me to confide in.

Yes, he was a human being in need. But, on the other hand, I'd brought my paper and wanted to catch on to what was happening in the world.

But how dare I avoid this simple call for help? I tried to frame a kind but not intrusive opening response, as the waitress placed a bowl before the man.

"Here are your cornflakes," she said.

That's what I get for living near Boston.

But the ship-in-the-harbor sentiment, and various *obbligati* on today being the first day of, et cetera, seemed to me, finally, to occur on too great a level of abstraction to be of any use, save in assuring the reader that "everything is fine."

But turning late into a ninety-degree corner at eighty miles an hour, everything is not, or does not seem, remotely fine. One is then in need of a more helpful axiom.

"Look where you want to go," the instructors said. At that ninety-degree bend, looking ahead of you reveals only a lack of road; accelerate to the breaking point, turn your head to look at the *apex* (or the clip point, as our friends the British say), and you'll both see where you want to go and steer the car there.

Not only is this good as "advice," per se, it actually works, while driving the car. *Because* it works, one begins to think ahead: "The process of driving a race is that of thinking backward from the turn before the longest straightaway."

Race car driving, at least in this initial introduction, comes down to cornering, and cornering, we are instructed, comes down to this formula: *radius = speed.*

The greater the radius, the greater the speed; so, the bigger radius turn you can make, the greater speed you can sustain. But (aha) the top speed sustainable through the greatest radius curve possible through ninety degrees is far inferior to aggregate speed-over-distance of a turn taken in two parts.

Part One: brake as late as possible on the *outside* (initial point) of the turn; turn *tightly*, at greatly reduced speed, into the turn (to the apex).

Part Two: accelerate in an *increasing radius turn* (speed increases as radius increases) toward the exit point (i.e., that

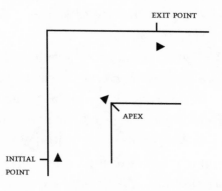

point at which one is back (a) on the straightaway and/or (b) setting up (aiming) for the initial point of the next turn).

This, to me, was great stuff, as it actually worked.

The difficulty increased geometrically with the rain.

That which we were instructed to drive (see diagram) was the "dry line," that is, that route upon which one would stay UNLESS IT WAS RAINING.

Now we were told, the line to adopt was (that's right) THE WET LINE.

The lines differed because of the rubber, oil, and muck left on the track.

This gook, when wet, turned those places subject to the greatest loss of rubber to ice. What were the places which had, above others, "heard the happy squealing"? The very initial points, apex, et cetera, we had been instructed to embrace.

So around the track we went, in cars with the instructors, as they pointed out the wet line to us, and we made many notes and nodded like german shepherd statues in the back window of Chevys as we tried to keep the notion clear. Until "wait a second," spoke up one of us: "All we've got to do is stay on the left."

Our instructor-driver pulled off the course, and spoke to his colleagues on the Motorola, and they decided to amend the syllabus. As all but one turn on the course was to the right, the answer was, in its Edison-like simplicity, simply stay on the left.

This made our understanding of the wet line easy, but our time spent in committee hell on earth, as the businessman who'd now solved the problems of *another* misguided operation appointed himself sage, commentator, and court jester for the remainder of the course; and the phrase "stay to the left," and its variants, rang in his recitation more frequently than "America" in the mouth of a politician.

I've got to hand it to the instructors. These fellows, in addition to being docents to the overly successful and bored, were working professional race drivers. They unquestionably loved the sport—they loved it sufficiently to delineate its entry-level mysteries to a bunch of (well, I have described us)—and they loved it sufficiently to abide WITH NO HINT OF EITHER ILL HUMOR, IMPATIENCE, OR CONDESCENSION the most boring, repetitious palaver I have ever heard on land or sea.

God bless them.

I see in my notes $15\,GR = (mph)^2$, that is, fifteen times the grip/radius = mph², and, beneath it, the notation *for the purposes of this introduction, we need only know that radius = speed.*

And I see my copy of their blackboard drawing of a car with a cup of coffee on its dashboard (the instructors used the motion of the liquid in the cup to illustrate the inertia and attitude of a car breaking and accelerating—accelerate, coffee goes back into your lap, rear tires compress; break, coffee goes forward onto the windshield, front tires compress) and the note that one must use coffee, and not cappuccino, as the foam invalidates the results.

Well, we drove around the course, and got our pictures took, and made a bunch of self-conscious bad jokes, perhaps like the fellow discovered with his niece. And I preferred it to the spa, as it didn't claim any wider personal or social applications.

It was just a bunch of middle-aged American guys learning to drive fast.

Domicile

There was, it seems to me, Greg's table, and there was the Italian Actor's house in Trastevere.

Greg's table was in his house on the next hill from ours up in Vermont.

He'd bought it from Annie during one of the periods in which she found herself in the antiques business. It was perfect.

It had been the preparation table in some country store near St. Johnsbury. It was six by three, thirty-five inches high, turned spruce legs, and a five-inch-thick maple butcher-board top.

It probably dated from the 1920s, and showed those seventy years of wear perfectly.

It was the center of Greg's kitchen. We'd sat there drinking daiquiris or coffee, gossiping or plotting, many days.

So when he announced he was selling the house, our grief and protestations were followed by the plea, "Sell us the table."

But it was not to be. A nice down-country couple had come up and seen his beautiful Civil War Cape and the view of that innumerable set of mountain ranges. They balked at the price and got all giddy over the table; one thing led to another. They stepped up, but the table stayed behind.

Now, the Italian Actor read a script of mine some years past, and indicated he was not averse to being wooed.

So I flew to Rome. I was invited to his house for lunch, and went to find a fellow around sixty, surrounded by loving family and faithful retainers—a view, perhaps, from one of the less xenophobic of the Victorians.

It was the most comfortable home—quiet and calm—and I longed for that sort of peace.

The trip to Rome was instructive. One of the man's retainers questioned me on the part, and, I am afraid, I treated his suggestions sufficiently lightly to inspire (as I imagine) a plotting rancor such as one might find delimited in one of the more xenophobic of the Victorians—in any case, the actor did not do the part (I was blessed, in the event, with Don Ameche). I did not inherit Greg's table, and an imminent New Arrival got us looking for a new home.

We looked for four years, and saw, I believe, upwards of eighty houses.

A late fiscal correction had rendered what seemed to be most of one particular suburb for sale, but we did not like it there.

yge

I recall one vast brick hulk, which was, in all particulars, unsuited to our needs.

The Realtor schlepped us out in any case, and showed us the two pools, and many-several wings, and other selling points, which made me homesick. Until we found ourselves on the back lawn. It was a lovely affair, and swept down to a brook. The scale of the thing, I believe, put me in mind of our backyard when I was a kid.

It was just swell. I stood musing on it—you know, the burning leaves, the snap of autumn cold through the muffler, the smell of the autumn childhood evening, and so forth, when I heard a screech like that of a trolley bisect the lawn at the dip I had taken for a stream and continue on its way into town.

"Excuse me," I said. "What was that?"

"That was the trolley," the Realtor said.

"The trolley runs through the backyard?" I said.

"Yes."

I paused.

"Wouldn't that," I asked, "discourage buyers?"

"Oh, no," she said, "only the nouveau riche would be upset by something like that."

Aha.

I love Realtors. I was in the business for a while myself as a child, and was reminded of the Lawrence of Arabia/ Gordon Liddy trick of holding one's hand in a flame. The Realtor's version of which is "Of course, it's wrong; the trick is not minding that it's wrong."

I do not think I have ever been shown a country house which did not abut a forest preserve, nor one in the city which was not just redone by an architect.

The trolley comment was the *ne plus ultra* and our favorite of Realtorisms. But we were charmed by recurrences in the vein of "It's too big"/"Board up the third floor" and "It isn't the neighborhood we want"/"You'll only be here in the evening."

I am, on the instant, capable of assuming and project-ing the appearance of grumpiness—any histrionic merit in such being moderated by the fact that at such times I am frothing with rage.

What can it do to one of my artistic temperament to be torn from what is probably napping but may in fact be composing important prose, to be torn, I say, and inveighed upon to see a home in all particulars inappropriate to my family's needs and my express instructions to the Realtor, harumph harumph? To be dragged through such an impos-sible, overpriced, ill-located, and graceless hulk and to be told, as the ultimate indignity: "But you'd have to act soon. It's already Under Offer."

Well, of course it's Under Offer. The phrase ranks with "I've never done this before" and "Yes, but I never inhaled" as one of the all-time punch lines.

"Ha ha ha, *kick* me," I would think each time I heard the phrase. "I know I am ridiculous. I am the old man with a new love. The love, in this case, is not even a house, but the *idea* of the new house. I am a sucker."

We traipsed in and traipsed out, learning that extra tad about human nature and saying, as I am sure others would say of us, "I can't believe people actually *live* this way."

But Then One Day (which is, of course, the beginning of

Act Two—Act One commencing Once Upon a Time, and Act Three, However, There Was One Thing They'd Forgotten).

And so in Act Two we locate the House. And, like our mother told us, We Just Knew.

Now, Jackie Mason told us that the Christian home is like a carpenter's shop—"See that bookcase? I made it myself"—while the Jewish is a loading dock: "You like that bookcase? It's *nothing*. It's going out. The new one'll be here in two weeks." And, yes, that's me all over.

So the only thing wrong with our dream house, it seems, was everything. J., my good friend in New York, has the most beautiful house I've ever seen. And well she might, as she is one of the most beautiful and elegant people in the world. It is an early-nineteenth-century jewel-box town-house, and her architect became ours, and as Act Two turned to Act Three I'd call her up and whine.

"Don't treat it like a house," she said. "Pretend it's a gigolo."

Genius advice. And so the house had to have everything *just so,* and so it was. Nothing was too good for that god-damned house.

Joseph Campbell tells us that the hero-journey begins with high spirits, hope, resolve, and glee, but soon metamorphoses into disgust and loathing.

Here is something I've noted: many people, at a first meeting in what may prove a difficult or adversarial relationship, will advertise themselves. That is, they will announce, if one listens closely, the method and extent to which they plan to exercise control.

Now why would they do that? They (and perhaps you and I) do that knowing that if the listener does not balk at the announcement, he or she is likely to accept the treatment advertised in docility.

I've had a producer, on a first meeting, tell me, "Yeah, I kept so-and-so waiting, and then arranged to have a masseuse rubbing me down when he showed up." Hmm.

I had a roofer come to give an estimate on a slate roof. "What sort of guarantee can you give?" I asked.

"Driveway," he said. "Driveway? What does that mean?" "Means if I get out the driveway fore the roof falls in, you're on your own," he said, and laughed at his good joke.

When we engaged the architect, he sent us a videotape. It was *Mr. Blandings Builds His Dream House.* So the reconstruction process went on. And I recalled the Rhine experiments in ESP.

Professor Rhine would have the subject guess the design on a card being held, out of sight, by an assistant. He said the only possible suggestion of ESP he found was this: in a small number of cases the subject guessed *wrong* a statistically improbably high number of times.

And I would say to the architect: "Why is it that each time a price differs from the estimate, it's *more* expensive?"

And he would sigh and look either wise or full of inexpressible pity, and the house is lovely, and the work is superb, and the contractor (G.F. RHODES CONST. BOSTON) did the job on time and on the money and with exquisite care and there you are.

We told our decorator that we'd like the place to be rather arts-and-crafts, and she kept showing us sketches which looked Brit., and then we discovered/realized/remembered that arts-and-crafts where she comes from means William Morris and Sanderson chintz, while on the American side it means Roycrofters, hammered copper, and *that* variety of rot, and you can add this, if you wish, to that same conversational story which holds, "They say 'pram' and we say 'baby carriage'; we say 'crib' and they say 'cot'," and suchlike, moldering since your youth.

I was looking for a house with a Grueby fireplace, and the date and the location of the neighborhood rendered me with something more than a fantasy. The neighborhood dates from 1870 to 1920 (ours is 1915), and the Grueby Faience Company was making tiles from the 1890s just a few miles away, the most beautiful tiles ever made.

I vowed I'd walk into a house and see the Grueby mantel and fireplace—a treasure unrealized by the sellers—and swoop up the dump on the spot. I didn't find the fireplace, but I did locate the Greg table up in Vermont. Scuttlebutt reported such at George's house on Route 2.

I drove by, found him in, and there was the exact kitchen preparation table, out in the barn. It had come originally from Jones's Country Store in East Montpelier, and George bought it in the fifties. He was using it as a reloading bench. I hemmed and hawed and was coy, and George was noncommittal, and I went back several times as if I was mustering the courage to ask him on a first date, and finally my advisors said, "Oh for God's sake, go in there with a check and ask him if he'd help you load it on the truck," which I did, and it now sits in our new kitchen.

Q. Do *things* make us happy?

A. I don't know.

I both would not and would like to think that they do.

I know that there is an anxiety to acquire, and an anxiety to disseminate, and there is the peace or absence of anxiety which can be heightened or perhaps even induced by clarity, proportion and grace in design, decor, and construction.

Or, to say it in American, it's real nice to live in a real nice house, which is not news but which is my grateful report.

December 24

I am in the locker room of a gym.

One of the men remarks that when he came in the place was empty, but now there's a *minyan* (a minimum of ten men, necessary for Jewish prayer).

I remark, "A logical place to find a *minyan* on Christmas Eve."

The fellow begins talking to a friend. He mentions he's been to see the play *Diary of Anne Frank,* and jokes, "No laughs. And I thought it was a comedy."

I joke, "To the Christians, it *is* a comedy."

The men laugh.

Walking out, it occurs to me that, in addition to being mildly amusing, my comment is, arguably, true.

The Comedy and the Romance end with the restoration of right order through the intervention of the God in the Machine.

In the original play, right order is restored when Anne announces that she believes that people are still good at heart. That is, in the time-honored phrase, "and then, she awoke to find it has all been a dream."

In the current adaptation, right order is restored when the Jews, the cause of all the commotion, are marched off to their deaths.

Is this a tragedy? No. For none of the characters' trials are engendered by their actions. Is it a drama? No, for it concerns itself with the mundane, and the end, therefore—torture and execution—is out of line with, disconsonant with, the tone, the stakes, the "situation" of the play as a whole.

The form in which this occurs (in which we see the intervention of a force of a different order of magnitude, which force comes from *without* the precincts of the play to Make All Right, in the traditional comedy, the realm of human behavior; in the *Diary*, from outside the attic) this form is the Comedy.

To take the least reliable of literary forms, the diary of an adolescent girl, and embrace it for its revelatory wisdom is perhaps other than wise. It is done in this case because we know that "in real life," the writer was killed.

If we forget for a moment that someone was killed, the form of the piece becomes more recognizable—it is *A Tree Grows in Brooklyn* or *Our Boardinghouse*, complete with (in the original) the traditional comedic punch line, "people are still good at heart" or "Waal, I guess we're all jes' *folks* . . ."

It is as mawkish to ascribe to the *Diary* literary worth as it would be to "appreciate" the pieced-together *menorot* of the camps as charming examples of woodcraft.

It is—one cannot even say "a truer understanding," for it is not for us to understand—but it is, I believe, the only possible approach or relationship to these artifacts, the only permissible relationship, to them, the *Diary* included, is silent, distanced respect. They are not and should not be "the possession of the world," nor should they be pressed into the world's service as entertainment.

I agree with Cynthia Ozick: Better the diary had been burned.

Late Season Hunt

New York was, of course, intolerable. I found that I was organizing my day around those times when it was possible—just possible—to get a cup of gourmet coffee without standing in line the otherwise requisite half hour.

But whose fault was it if not my own, who'd chosen luxury and fashion (at least for the fall) over a healthy life in the outdoors? And I wasn't writing a word of any worth, and, to complete the indictment, I was frittering away yet another deer season.

Vermont archery was over, as was centerfire rifle; and Morris, my neighbor down the road, had gotten a 175-pound buck in the orchard just across from my house.

And I had just turned fifty.

My friend and hunting companion Bob turned fifty some five or six years ago.

He was and is an outdoorsman, a hunter, trapper, and forester—he had, his wife reported, spent his fiftieth year complaining and full of crotchets about encroaching Old Age. But when the clock ticked over onto fifty, he was cured, and went back to an uncomplaining, aggressively active life.

I had spent my fiftieth year emulating him. And now I had turned fifty and found myself still the slave of habit, sloth, and urban depravity, as the deer season waned, and I had to get out of town.

I thought I'd look for an adventure somewhat greater than tripping around the backyard, but not quite as Herculean as going to Maine. (Maine, of course, bars hunting on Sundays, which always seemed to me an unfortunate survival of "the King's Deer"). So I contacted Uncle Jammers Guides (Jim Ehlers), out of Sugarbush, Vermont, and he told me he'd put me on some tracks up in the Northeast Kingdom, and I'd go to the Kingdom, for the last days of blackpowder, muzzle-loading season.

I flew from New York to Burlington, Vermont, and drove to Plainfield, to the River Run Restaurant, for lunch.

Jimmy Kennedy was in the kitchen. He made me bacon and eggs and reminded me to take along a safety pin on the hunting trip. What for? For a touchhole pick.

Friend of his, he said, had a safety pin, and it saved the day, on a blackpowder shoot, when the touchhole in his rifle clogged. Great idea.

I remember old Pennsylvania guns, with a hole bored in the forestock, right below that for the ramrod, and in the hole was carried a long quill to clean out the touchhole.

I remembered hunting with blackpowder shooters in east Texas, sitting around in the evening at Bill Bagwell's forge, discussing the contributions blackpowder shooting had made to the language: "hang fire"; "flash-in-the-pan"; "lock, stock, and barrel"; "skinflint"; "keep your powder dry"; "shot his rod" (corrupted into "wad"); "chew the rag"; "spruce up" ("sprues up," i.e., with the sprue—which is the nonspherical portion of the cast ball, that portion left when the molten lead overflows the mold—up, that is, pointed toward the muzzle); and (which prompted this reflection) "ramrod," used as a verb.

So much of the appeal of field sports, at least to me, who practices them infrequently, is the gear and the language pertinent to the thing. I get out there only several days a year, but I, along with the legion of my sedentary coeval enthusiasts, am always up for an outdoorsy book or catalogue (anything's better than playing golf).

And here I was, being reminded—as does blackpowder shooting in general—that the simplest gear is the best, the simplest gear, in this case, being a safety pin.

Jimmy and I spoke about ice fishing for a while; I paid my check and headed out to my house.

My first stop was up at my cabin, to pick up my gear.

I took down my .58 Hawken, and cleaned it. I blew through the barrel, but I found it clogged. I pulled the nipple and saw the lube had set up in the touchhole, and that, happy day, I could clean it out using a safety pin. I cleaned the nipple, cleaned the bore, polished the thimbles, got the whole thing shining, and I went outside and set up a target at fifty yards.

That's a pretty good range, as (a) it's going to be about the limit of any shot in the woods and (b) it's a range I can actually hit at.

I put a couple of half-inch red Targ-A-Dots on the cardboard, and put my first shot two inches left and on for elevation. With a second shot I obliterated the Targ-A-Dot, and felt about as good as I'd felt since I first went down to the City, the rifle exhibiting a degree of forgiveness positively feminine.

I was standing out there, waxing rhapsodic about the blackpowder rifle, its excellencies, its forgiving nature, its lack of recoil, and its general friendliness, when the sun went down. I cleaned my gun by the oil lamp, hurried back to the house, threw much too much gear into a pack, and got into the pickup for the drive to Sugarbush.

I remembered a cold and hungry Vermont holiday season, thirty-plus years before. I was out of work, and heard of an opening for an experienced bartender at the Sugarbush Inn.

I called and made an appointment for an interview. I went to the Montpelier Library and found *Old Mr. Boston's Bartenders Guide,* and studied it night and day until the date of my interview, when that person upon whom I had counted for a lift to Sugarbush disappointed me, and I sat out the remainder of the holiday season hungry, cold, and grumbling.

The awful thing about not winning an Academy Award is this: you don't get to give your speech. It just rather sits there and festers.

"Yes," you think, "it's alright that I lost. That's only fair, and that's the game. But there *must* be some way that, *hāving* lost, I can still mount the podium and give my most excellent and philosophical speech."

But no. And neither did I ever get to display my (granted, theoretical) excellence as a bartender.

And never before had I gotten to Sugarbush, that momentary Oz of my youth. I'd gotten as far north as Hyde Park, for the odd auction, and several times to Johnson, to the Johnson Woolen Mills Store, but never to Sugarbush.

I arrived at the Snow Ridge Inn. A young woman told me that everyone was out snowmobiling, and that I could fling my stuff into one of the cabins and work out the details of my stay later on.

I think snowmobiling, at least in Vermont, contains the story of a particularly American triumph.

In my youth, up there, in the turbulent sixties, snowmobilers had the reputation of being rowdies—outlaw bikers on ice, bent on inebriation, vandalism, and whatever mischief one could get into whilst wrapped like a puff pastry at forty below.

But their image was changed, and changed by the most unusual of tactics—they changed their image by changing their actions.

Makes one think.

This reversal, this embrace (in fact, championship) of accountability, safety, and good neighborliness, happened, as I understand, largely under the direction of the Vermont Snowmobile Club, founded and first presided over by Chuck Barnett.

Chuck was the longtime postmaster of my town in Vermont.

I had the privilege of chatting with him many mornings, not only about the weather but about the woods, the state of the world, and, should conversation flag, his coonhounds, which were kenneled at his house, next to the post office, and whose song was regularly heard.

And so the management, as I have said, was out snowmobiling, and I drove the pickup over to my cabin.

There it was. No phone. No television. Privacy. And I was alone.

I could enter and spread out and check and moon over my gear, I could sleep till dawn the next morning, I could open the windows, accountable to no one. I could live, for the moment, a free man.

I lugged my gear up on the porch, and opened the door. I looked down, and at my feet was a note: "Call Norman Lear Immediately."

Well, then, I was strong enough to get myself out of New York, but I was not strong enough not to call Norman Lear immediately. He told me he was working on a project and I was the only one to write it, and other irresistible flattery, and I made an appointment to meet with him the next week, back in New York.

For, yes, *of course* I was a fraud. Whom was I attempting to kid?

As there was no one there but myself, I sussed that answer out fairly quickly. But was I not, on the other hand, nevertheless entitled to Go Hunting?

Yes. I put away my gear, and went out to meet Jim and Nathan for dinner, and we made a plan.

The plan was this: we'd meet at the Snow Ridge at five-thirty, and drive up to Wenlock, the preserve up by Island Pond. Fine.

I went shopping down in the town: tea, butter, eggs, bread, cheese, and ham.

I went back to my cabin, and fell asleep. The radio woke me at five to some symphonic music. I took a quick shower, dashed into the kitchen to make breakfast, and a perfect sandwich (eggs, butter, cheese, bread, ham), put it inside several wax paper bags, closed it with a rubber band, and Jim and Nathan arrived.

I had, of course, high hopes for that rubber band. It was to fix my filled-out deer tag to my fallen buck. It, like the safety pin, was to be the talisman signifying my foresight, and would, therefore, insure an increased promise of success.

It was not to be.

I am a bad rifle shot and an inexperienced, inept (but happy) hunter.

Larry Benoit, the king of hunters (*How to Bag the Biggest Buck Of Your Life*) writes—and experience proves you've got to get out there *every day*—you have to know what the woods look like before you start remarking the magnificently camouflaged animal standing there.

It seems to me a lot like writing. One may only write an hour a day, but that hour can't be scheduled in advance. It may come as part of a day devoted to reading, or napping, or skyving off, but the writer has to spend a lot of time alone and quiet before he's capable of recognizing the difference between an idea and a good idea.

Larry Benoit also wrote the way to get a monster buck is to follow a merely large buck and, when you get your shot, let the buck go.

This seems to me to equal Hemingway's advice, to write the best story you can and then throw out all the good lines—best advice I ever read about writing.

And here we are up in Larry Benoit country, up where the big bucks are.

Nathan and James and I are crammed into the front seat of an old pickup, drinking vast travel mugs of coffee, driving two hours up to the Wenlock preserve, and talking about fishing.

Jim says the thing about fishing is that you learn something new *all* the time, how there's always something new to be learned. They compose a paean to ice fishing and I want nothing more than to go.

We drive past Orleans and they talk about the spawning trout jumping the dam up there.

Nathan begins talking about his Uncle Dwane, who's meeting us in Island Pond; about how he's *always* learning from the deer; about how Dwane's passed that or is passing that down to him, Nathan; and about how much there is to learn. This is a constant and, to me, invigorating instructive, and grateful quality of outdoors people—their reverence for knowledge and their understanding that knowledge lies not in the self but in the world around them (and if I get philosophic I had better take myself ice fishing and let it burn off).

We rendezvous with Dwane in Island Pond. Another coffee. We begin talking, for some reason, about traveling.

Dwane's been on the road. With what, I ask; and it turns out he's in antiques. Not only is he in antiques, he and Nathan are relatives of the late Albert May, THE MAN WHO WEARS THE DERBY HAT, of Molly's Pond, Vermont.

I used to go to Albert's auctions Saturday nights, back in the mid-sixties.

He was the quintessential entertainer, he knew his material, he knew his audience, and he loved being up there, and they loved him for it.

He would auction off a bag of clothespins and then say that he had "just one more," and sell *that,* and be surprised that it seemed there was just one more. And he'd sell clothespins for an hour.

Dwane said one time there was some hippie from the college down the road came to the auction; and the hippie, not finding a chair, had perched himself in the tree outside the auction shed. Well, fine, but he was dressed in the tatters of that clan and that day. His clothes were rags, and his genitals hung down through a rent in his jeans.

Albert espied him and remarked to the crowd that it beat all of his knowledge of nature, how early the squirrels were putting nuts in the trees.

It was still early, it was not quite light. We ordered up more coffee and talked about the old estate auctions, the old farms broken up, the antique business.

(I once found a .32 Winchester Low Wall, first year of manufacture [1885] for twenty-five dollars, covered in rust, but cleaned up fine.)

They cleaned it up for me at Orvis, brought back the exterior metal (the bore was fine) and polished up the wood. Lovely little rifle.

Into the buttstock some early owner had carved his initials: c.k. It hung on its return from Orvis, for a short time, right above my desk, until my good friend and hunting companion Chris Kaldor stopped by one day and took the gun down to examine it. He and I both registered the initials at the same time. Chris, gentleman that he is, handed the rifle back and remarked about the weather, and the Low Wall, the next week, and after some extraordinary soul-searching on my part, went where it (obviously) was destined.

Dwane said the glory years of the farm auction were gone, that one was more apt to find a treasure, if one found it at all, at a sale out of a condo—in Vermont or, more likely, in Florida, where the old folks had gone.

I'd always wanted to know, and I asked him: How's it happen that *any* of the great pieces at an auction find their way past the auctioneer? He said that was the great art of the auction business—that the dealer, trying to get the job from the householders, had to strike the balance between keeping the cream for himself and leaving enough of interest in the auction to attract the buyer; that the great part of the auctioneer's art was the first negotiation, and the actual auction just the sideshow to clear out the house.

The whole thing not unlike the movie business.

But then we'd had enough coffee, and it was up the mountain.

We found the logging road Dwane and Jim had scouted, and we cut the track of a buck.

I was given the lead, and started packing all of my useless

gear onto my belt and back. Dwane suggested that the deer weren't going to wait while I festooned myself, and I acknowledged the logic of his position by watching my rifle fall apart.

"Works all year, but not up here," the old phrase has it.

The wedge, which keeps the barrel in the stock and which had never in a decade budged without my deliberate intervention, dropped straight out of my rifle and into the snow.

Well, we found it, and pounded it back in with the hilt of a knife, and I was ready to set out when the rawhide holding my "possibles" bag onto its cunning Period shoulder strap shredded and my bag fell in the snow.

The bag was a loss, so I decanted powder patch and ball into two plastic speedloaders, stuffed them, a full capper, my third spare compass, and a candy bar into the various pockets of my old red Johnson coat, and nodded to my similarly ready fellow hunters.

Meet back here in four hours, Jim said. Road runs north and south, you're going up the mountain. West, come back to the road. All you got to do is walk east.

Excellent. Up the mountain I went, tracking the buck in the snow.

He went here, he went there, he eventually cut back east, onto the road, walked the road for a while, and jumped down into the low land down below. He played me like a violin. He found some old tracks and walked in them, he jumped from one old set onto another, he'd spring down a little hill, and he was *never* walking fast—he had a City Boy behind him, and his flight was a necessary but nontaxing academic exercise.

My morning was a bit more strenuous. The buck ran me down and up, across the road and up the mountain, and then it was noon, and I'd been tracking him over four hours, and I was drenched to the skin, and cold.

My legs were shaking as I went down the mountain. I hit the road and guessed the truck was to my left and turned left.

I met Nathan, and we split my sandwich, which he pronounced excellent.

We went back for lunch to Island Pond.

I changed into the spare silk underwear I had (in about my only display of hunting savvy) brought along. My shirt and coat were soaked through.

I went next door to the gun store and bought a new green and black Johnson (short) jacket and one of their shirts, pretty glad to be warm. I went back to the café and hung up my sweat-soaked long red coat.

I love that coat. I've hunted and worked, and walked and slept under it the statutory twenty years, and it always proves to be too heavy, tracking a deer. It's fine for sitting on a cold stand, but when you start moving it's too warm, too long, and has too many pockets into which I've put too much useless stuff. Well, I suppose I have not quite mastered that lesson yet.

James suggested a change of scene. (I think he took his cue from my physical state.) He said he knew a good spot to wait out a buck at sundown.

So we got back into the pickup and I slept the deepest sleep of my life two hours back to Sugarbush.

The sun was just going down, we had that extra half

hour of legal hunting. We walked through a field of thigh-high snow. The moon started to rise.

Jim put me in the corner of a field. I sat the last half hour still as a log, and saw nothing. We walked back in the dark to the pickup truck.

We had a bourbon at the Sugarbush Inn. I went back to the cabin and slept fourteen hours.

We spent the next day hunting around Johnson.

It had turned cold and was blowing sleet.

We were in fairly flat country and Jim said that they most probably bedded down around a given-up orchard he knew.

He and Nathan walked in to start them and put me on the inside and back from them, that is, they planned to drive the deer across my path.

To hunt deer in thick woods in a snowstorm is one of the most beautiful, the happiest, things that I know. I was enjoying it so much that I missed the deer.

They'd passed right before me, twenty yards out.

We got on their trail and kept on it several hours, and then I was played out. There was a half hour left of the season. We went back into the woods, I stopped on the edge of a small clearing, the sun came out. I just sat there, delighted.

What a successful hunt.

I kept up for a couple of days, and told myself it was not a bad performance for a dissipated city fellow with a desk job. I drank some good bourbon in Sugarbush, and re-membered that cold winter thirty years ago.

I fell asleep three nights in a row at eight P.M. and remem-bered what it is like to sleep well. I'd had a moment by myself. A very good way to celebrate the transition of my fiftieth birthday.

James, Nathan, and I shot at a stump some thirty yards off to clear the guns. I drove home, cleaned the Hawken, hung it in the cabin, and flew back to New York.

As a hunter, of course, I am a fraud. But it was a hell of a good vacation.

Acknowledgment

David Daiches, *Scotch Whisky: Its Past and Present*